D1485922

CONCRETE IDEAS:
material to shape a city

CONCRETE IDEAS:

material to shape a city

edited by Pina Petricone

foreword by George Baird
contributions by Jürgen Mayer H., Sarah Iwata, Graeme Stewart,
Will Bruder, George Elvin, and Mark West
afterword by Charles Waldheim

contents:

acknowledgements

Pina Petricone

This book would not have been possible without the generous support of the Canadian Cement Association, as well as George Baird and the John H. Daniels Faculty of Architecture, Landscape and Design. Pivotal to its formation were the tireless commitment and immense talents of Sarah Iwata and Alessia Soppelsa. As managing editors, they brought it all together and never allowed their 'critical eye' to stray. Their work was enabled by the pivotal support of Courtney Meagher, Zita da Silva D'Alessandro and Jacqueline Raaflaub. I am indebted to contributors George Baird, Mark West, Graeme Stewart, Charles Waldheim, Sarah Iwata, Will Bruder, George Elvin and Jürgen Mayer H., who shared their expertise to help work through the sometimes difficult-to-express objectives of this book. Each of their unique approaches to ubiquitous concrete allowed for its multiple new readings. I must acknowledge the indispensable work and contributions of the studio participants, Gary Chien, Tangie Genshorek, Vanessa Graham, Jessica Grebenc, Jennifer Haliburton, Leigh Jeneroux, Shirley Lee, Anne Miller, Shi Ning, Alessia Soppelsa, Kenzie Thompson, Liam Woofter, and Eric van Ziffle. Their insightful responses to this unconventional research project became the seeds for this book. Thank you to studio critics Barry Sampson, Robert Levit, Shadi Rhabaran, Scott Sorli, Betsy Williamson, Will Bruder and Brigitte Shim for giving 'fuel' to the students' 'fire' and for the imagination they brought to the subject matter. I would be remiss not to acknowledge the pivotal and enabling contributions of Oscar Riera Ojeda and his team, Leo Malinow, Alejandra Román, and Yanina Arabena. Oscar's ability to 'see' and his appreciation of the subtleties of *Concrete Ideas* transformed its promise into reality. Finally, I must thank Anita Matusevics for her generosity, which has allowed this book to benefit from her enormous talent; Rodolphe el-Khoury, for his quiet but immeasurable support of my work; and, Ralph Giannone, for his clear seeing and 'brutal honesty', which has made all the difference.

foreword

George Baird

George Baird, Dean Emeritus,
*John H. Daniels Faculty of Architecture,
Landscape, and Design.*

The history of concrete and its role in architecture is a long one, stretching from ancient Rome to the present. But perhaps the most significant aspect of that history for this volume of essays and proposals is the disrepute into which it fell in the 1970s. Following the setting in of some doubt in regard to the durability that could be expected of the celebrated 'white architecture' of the 1920s, a number of architects – but most especially Le Corbusier – began in the 1930s to experiment with concrete – both in cast-in-place and in precast forms. In the first instance, this led to the creation of a whole series of remarkable works by him, stretching from the Unite d'habitation in Marseilles through to the new capital in Chandighar.

In the second instance, however, it led to a whole series of works by architects throughout the world, which emulated the work of the great Le Corbusier, but which resulted in works of considerably less visual potency. Probably the most telling brief account of that dissipation of cultural power is the one published by Robert Venturi in the 1972 polemic he published with colleagues: *Learning from Las Vegas*. The damning essay was entitled: 'From La Tourette to Neiman-Marcus', and it depicted that decline in a powerfully graphic way. From roughly that point onward, concrete took on increasingly negative cultural connotations in architecture, and the public-at-large gradually developed a substantial antipathy towards it.

That antipathy is one of the important starting points for the group of authors and creators whose works have been assembled by Pina Petricone in this volume. Her and their inventive ideas and proposals may well have the capacity to contribute to a new legitimization of this venerable, but often controversial building material.

Professor Petricone has brought an engaging group of participants together here. It includes the group of students at the Daniels Faculty that worked with her in a studio option focusing on the new design possibilities that have opened up for concrete, as well as Graeme Stewart and Sarah Iwata, two notable recent graduates of the faculty. In addition the volume includes statements by two different visitors to the Faculty that were holders of the Frank O. Gehry International Visiting Chair in Architectural Design. These were Will Bruder, who served as Gehry Chair during the academic year 2006-2007 and Jurgen Mayer H. who succeeded him the following year. Then, in turn, the statements of Bruder have been joined by those of Professor George Elvin, Director of the Green Technology Forum, and Professor Mark West of the University of Manitoba, so well-known for his continuing material explorations that range from structural analysis to poetry.

introduction

Pina Petricone

Concrete doesn't lie. It captures, registers then exposes the minutia of detail and texture of the interior of its form, offering for Modernist architecture the requisite uncovered 'naked-ness' and therefore moral 'honesty' to represent the inhibitions of the movement. An unruly mass of coagulated, colourless gravel, raw concrete learns to speak only as it reacts to its mould. One might argue that concrete is as concrete does, and as the most used material in the world, after water,[1] what it *does* is present itself ubiquitously across the built environ-ment. In all its abundance, it has become generalized as grey, unnatural, light absorbing, and heavy, slipping easily into our urban subconscious as a particular, inexpressive fabric of cities. Still today it has an overwhelming negative association with the 'cheap and easy' brutal examples of the 1960s and 70s generally misunderstood and disliked. The philoso-pher Mark Kingwell urges us to take a second look, and to "go out and touch some…run your hands along the spongy almost smooth surface…skim your fingers over a few of the thousand small holes…" in order to have the opportunity to see concrete properly. In his urban construct, *Concrete Reveries*, Kingwell dares to say "if you treat concrete well, it will reveal new layers of possibility, new aspects of beauty."[2]

Concrete Ideas presents a body of material research that attempts to make claims about concrete's inherent expression and its inevitable shift in cultural status provoked by invisible but transforming current nano-technologies.

It is now common knowledge that de-polluting nanocoatings can be applied to concrete surfaces to make them smog-eating machines. Photocatalytic titanium dioxide nanopar-ticles trap and then decompose airborne pollutants — all in a few thousandths of an inch. This kind of invisible treatment of concrete entirely inverts some of its fundamental and rec-ognizable qualities as does super-thin almost ductile high-performing and de-constructible prefabricated concrete, or the engineered cement composites that make them 500 percent more resistant to cracking under severe loads or in extreme environments. We must ask then, to what extent do these nanotechnologies impact on the slow shift in the cultural and aesthetic status of concrete, which until very recently carried inherent implications of an unforgiving, unsustainable heaviness.

With a group of graduate architecture students at the University of Toronto we contemplat-ed this question among other material speculations, which look abroad to ultimately test ar-guments within the concrete-dense case of Toronto, Canada. If we can say there still exists a general perception that concrete looks best, from the outside, in Mediterranean climates, an argument to the contrary can be found in our minus 30°C to plus 30°C Toronto, where sun angles can reach only 23° in winter,[3] which has an unparalleled richness of shining moments in concrete — ones which do not fit the decidedly beautiful sculptural and smooth moulds of celebrated concrete buildings around the world. The question is, can we find virtue in the unique qualities of (lack of) smoothness, in greyness and in a sublime ugliness?

Finally, *Concrete Ideas* proposes that a more self-conscious tectonic innovation and expression of the material, as strategic interventions of infrastructure, building and surface, can afford new presence to existing concrete architectures by providing a lens through which we can perceive and experience them.

The book and its project research is divided into five *-ion* parts: abstraction, operation, insertion, section, and speculation. Prefaced by an illustrated inventory of select, current concrete nano-technologies, each chapter presents the city-building active agents implicit in *abstraction*, *operation*, *insertion*, *section*, and *speculation* as they pertain to concrete in its existing as well as projected form. Each chapter delves progressively further into depths of hypothetical urban intervention to eventually declare a kind of tectonic urbanism tested on six strategic sites, primed to forge new urban links, and considered through a 'scaffold' of explicit global lessons.

In the midst of these questions, Graeme Stewart looks to the past for solutions for the future. Stewart 'unpacks' the cultural status of now aged international style apartment blocks, abundant in North America, and planted in Russia, the UK and Hong Kong; and speculates on how technological restorations can lead to new architectures which in turn have the power to shape new identities. This potential is remarked on by Jürgen Mayer's '45°', which supports his suspicions that a general shift from an elemental International Style towards a sculptural understanding of architecture and space was made possible by new developments in concrete. Sarah Iwata's 'Concrete Climate' looks instead not to the limitations, but to the liberations of weather and its 'partnerships' with technology to blur the defining boundaries between infrastructure, building and surface.

Similarly, the resulting studio experiments present innovative tectonic strategies, at various scales, to positively inform the cultural, aesthetic and sustainable status of this age-old material. Buildable solutions are framed by BÉTON-BRUT/BÉTON-DOUX, photo interpretations of the Toronto case; annotated by WINDCHILL TO HUMIDEX, average and extreme local temperatures and precipitation each year from 1954 (the earliest year of Toronto brutalism) to 2008; and, finally challenged perhaps by the following four fundamental provocations:

If material is a form of thinking in architecture, what constitutes material research that is outside more conventional questions of technology and experiments rather with questions of authority, perception and aesthetic culture?

Can a material such as concrete be categorically described as 'cold' as it is so often accused of being, likely for its utilitarian (vein or grain-less) renditions? The definition seems to depend on the inherent psychology rather than the inherent performance of the material. How can we experiment with the complexity of these tectonic expressions of the material?

Given the now mainstream nanotechnologies that transform the performance of materials at the molecular level without fundamentally changing the material aesthetic, can we anticipate a shift in its cultural status? Ultimately, concrete might look the same but is no longer burdened by its unsustainable, gravity-ridden heaviness.

Can we affect the general disregard or 'forgettable-ness' of 1960s and 1970s Brutal concrete stock which do not fit the decidedly beautiful, sculptural, and smooth moulds of celebrated concrete buildings around the world by finding virtue in unique qualities of (lack of) smoothness, in greyness and in ugliness?

When Will Bruder, George Elvin and Mark West, three diverse leading experimenters in concrete, contemplate in their work these ultimate presumptions of *Concrete Ideas*, we appreciate the complexities of the material's aesthetic treatise. Bruder directly asks: "Just because we can, do we do it? Why would concrete ever want to be translucent?" He explains how concrete is not just a poor man's stone. It is a material which gains its richness through ideas – regardless of whether it's a simple concrete block from the 1970s or the *Agilia* of the 21st C. Elvin searches, on the other hand, for the way in which a material such as concrete might escape its historic perception as the heavy, massive bulk that holds things up, as it becomes imbued with the ability to do so many other things. The nature of concrete, the most commonplace material in the world, is not inherent anymore. West then argues that the inherent psychology of a material is not divorced from the performance of the material. And, although a material at any given time is prodigiously active, its performance so to speak is derived not so much by its technological or biological composition, but rather almost entirely by its mould.

The physical sensation of rough, board-formed concrete on skin segues Charles Waldheim's afterword, 'Brutal Memories', which convincingly builds an argument for *Concrete Ideas*' "generational rebuttal to the arguments against modernism." The conflation of material, meaning, and memory is unravelled in support of our aim to ultimately explore the anticipated shifts in appreciation of concrete. We reconsider this age-old building material as supple, light, and instrumental in the re-presentation of existing concrete citizens and, in turn, the re-formation of its city.

1. Larfarge Conference Proceedings - 2008: "Solid States: Changing Time for Concrete" conference in New York (www.lafarge.com/wps/portal/3_4_2-Partenariats)
2. Mark Kingwell, *Concrete Reveries: Consciousness and the City* (Toronto: Penguin Group Viking Canada, 2008) pp.4-6
3. National Research Council Canada www.nrc-cnrc.gc.ca

ABSTRACTION

-noun
'an impractical idea; something visionary
and unrealistic'

'abstraction,' definition #3. Dictionary.com, Random House

It has always seemed curious that elaborating the definition of concrete to include 'pertaining to or concerned with realities or actual instances rather than abstractions'[1] admits a kind of idiosyncrasy when the realness, so to speak, of its noun lends itself so willingly to the Modernist powers of abstraction. The material concrete seemed to be as much about the quintessence of modernity as the architecture it defined and gave rise to. Nowhere is this expressed more clearly than in the New Brutalism Movement, coined by the Smithsons, arguably derived from Le Corbusier's use of raw concrete, béton-brut, for the exposed finish of poured-in-place concrete buildings whose concrete surface bears the imprint of the forming process. Le Corbusier's decision to leave the concrete in its rough, abstracted state immediately imbued it with the requisite Modernist ideology of honest 'nudity' – liberating it from cumbersome historical or decorative particulars. With this 'invention' of béton-brut, Le Corbusier gave new cultural meaning to a conventional construction practice. Later, Reyner Banham's *The New Brutalism: Ethic or Aesthetic?* asks whether this implied pragmatic honesty or 'ethical utilitarianism' of the 1950s and 1960s exposed concrete buildings, whose registered formwork is either smooth (machined), exaggerated (bush hammered) or carries traces of the fallible human hand that built it, can also express an inherent aesthetic.

We must ask then, if the inherent aesthetic of brutalist concrete is susceptible to a new reading when fore-grounded by a new concrete – one which might look the same, but behaves differently.

1. 'Concrete,' definition #2, Dictionary.com, Random House.

1966 **Clorindo Testa** machined precast panels render the façade like lace,
Buenos Aires, Argentina a kind of textile

2005

PERIPHERIQUES
Architectes
Paris, France

the atrium screen is reconsidered in super-thin
precast concrete

Agilia®
super fluid concrete

Agilia® concrete uses superplasticizers to reduce the water content and make a super viscous medium. Pumped with a hydraulic hose, gravity levels the concrete and eliminates the need for additional vibration. The resultant finish is incredibly smooth, which reduces the finishing time required by 75%.

"Agilia® offers a robust solution based on granular packing concepts and on the latest discoveries in organic chemistry, mineral chemistry and fluid mechanics applied to fresh concrete. Strict control of mix design technology enables optimal application of cement properties and allows Agilia® to retain its slump for up to two hours...Setting time is controlled and early strength is comparable to conventional concrete."

Agilia Brochure
Lafarge

Inside the smooth undulated Agilia® concrete volume of the recently completed Saint-Pierre de Firminy Church originally designed by Le Corbusier.

Bendable Concrete
engineered cement concrete

Engineered cement composites, or bendable concrete, is more flexible, thus less likely to fail under stress, and lighter and more durable than traditional concrete. Instead of using gravel aggregate, coated polyvinyl alcohol fibres and extremely fine silica sand are used to increase the concrete's bending ability. Reducing the need for steel allows for freer, more curvaceous forms and possible shapes as well as improving earthquake resistance.

"Will the infrastructure of tomorrow be sustainable and built in harmony with the natural environment? It may be difficult to meet these challenges with current brittle concrete, no matter what the compressive strength is. Materials like ECC, with its ultra ductility and tight crack width control, however, show characteristics that may meet the demands of next generation infrastructure."

Dr. Victor C. Li
The University of Michigan, Ann Arbor, USA
Engineered Cementitious Composites

Laboratory testing measures degrees of pliability in bendable concrete.

Ceracem®
ultra high performance concrete

Sika and Eiffage Construction have combined to research and develop Ceracem®, a ductile ultra-high performance concrete offering remarkable aesthetic possibilities. This new material, available as a cold-formable ceramic cement, is derived from BSI developed by Eiffage at the end of the 1990s. BSI concrete uses micro fibres embedded in its mix to achieve compressive strengths of up to 175 MPa and tensile strengths of 8 to 10 MPa. Without the need for passive reinforcement, BSI structural elements can be cast to less than an inch thick. Such dense material requires up to three times less concrete, can be used to span greater distances and is impermeable to corrosion from abrasion and chemicals. In addition, no additional heat treatments or vibration is necessary to cure BSI concrete.

"Ceracem concrete offers solutions with advantages such as speed of construction, improved aesthetics, superior durability, and impermeability against corrosion, abrasion and impact, which translates to reduced maintenance and longer life span for the structure. With this type of concrete it is possible to reduce or eliminate passive reinforcement and the thickness of the concrete elements can be reduced, which results in material and cost savings."

Baha Abdelrazig
Sika Regional Technology, Support Centre
Asia Pacific, Malaysia

Fibre reinforced BSI concrete
shown in SEM photo.

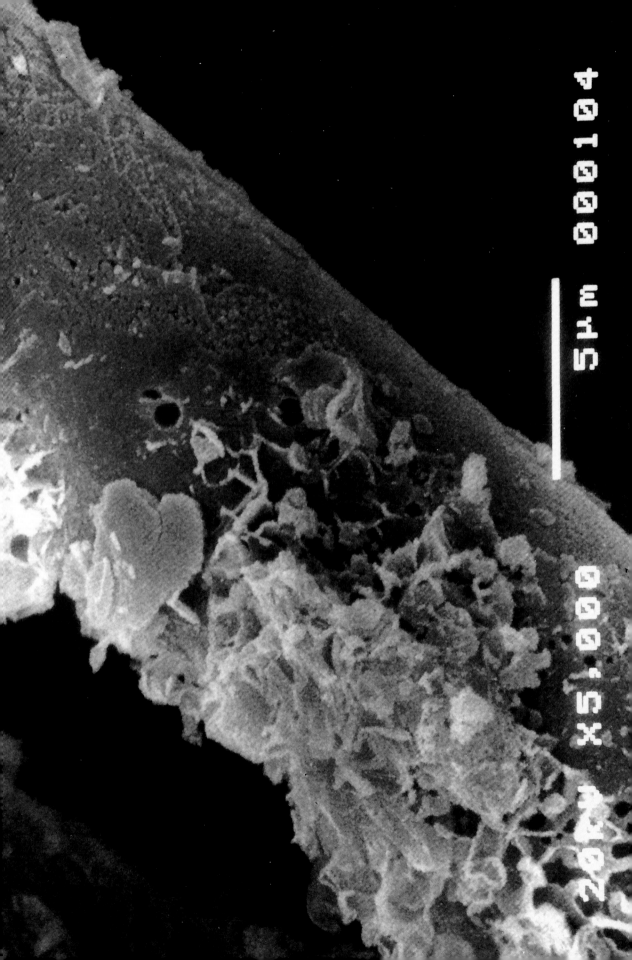

45°

Jürgen Mayer H.

Sometime in the 1970s there
seemed to be a common
agreement between architects
and clients to introduce the
45° angle on most corners
of a building; as detail, as
mega form and as ornament
– an international design
element that no-one has so
far written about.

It is my suspicion that this shift from an element/component based International Style towards a sculptural understanding of architecture and space was made possible by new developments in concrete.

The hierarchy of floor, wall and ceiling was blurred by a seemingly humble continuation of surface from horizontal to angled to vertical orientation. The 'oblique' as theorized by Paul Virilio and Claude Parent might have been one aspect of strategizing architecture as a non-directional, non-hierarchical envelope.

Yet, in everyday architecture what remained was a chamfered corner until the 1990s when new software technology made even more complex organic shapes possible. What we see in the 1970s 45° angles is a preamble to architecture in the late 1990s and the 21st century, a first test run for the potential of exposed concrete.

In most cities around the world, as in Berlin today, we can still find some 45° angles on buildings which represent the sculptural idea of an architectural surface continuum. However, this layer of modern architecture might soon disappear!

Shirley Lee
Abstraction of CN Tower

notes on abstraction

In the years between the mid-1950s and the mid-1970s
the City of Toronto experienced remarkable accelerated
growth. During this period of immense prosperity,
concrete provided the ideal qualities of efficiency,
cost effectiveness, and a forward-looking modernity
appropriate to this 'adolescent' North American city.
This unparalleled collection of idealized concrete
abstractions grew to punctuate the predominant
stone and brick building fabric with a familiar
presence that has somehow now slipped back into
our urban subconscious.

Abstraction of
Sheraton Centre

Alessia Soppelsa

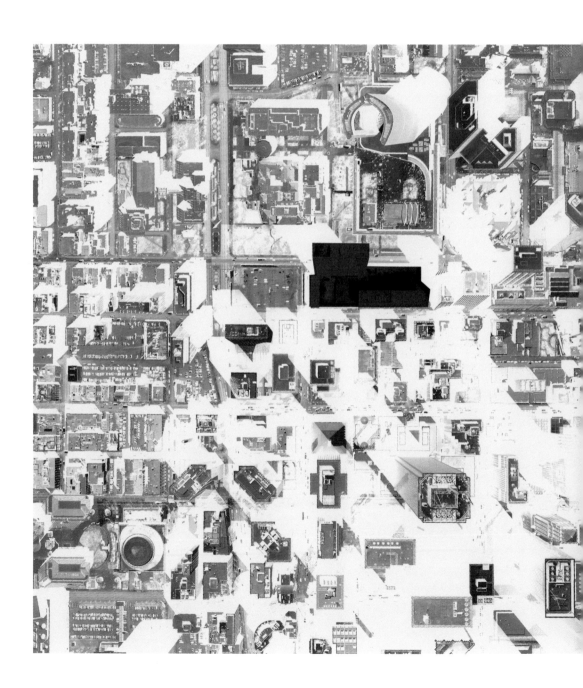

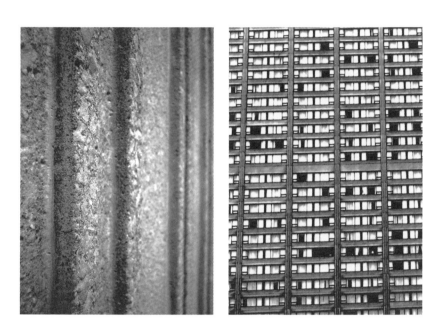

Degrees of abstraction through repetition and the relentless fine grain of corduroy precast panels that render the mass of an exposed concrete building arguably afford it monumental status. Soppelsa's photographic abstractions of the Sheraton Centre, often referred to as a mountainous out-cropping, built in 1972 to flank the open side of the infamous Nathan Phillips Square, are meant to simultaneously document, analyze and interpret its quintessential brutal façade. The massive centre was always meant to provide a complementary context against which the ultra modern square and City Hall were to be read.

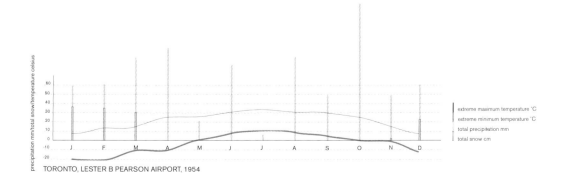

TORONTO, LESTER B PEARSON AIRPORT, 1954

Abstraction of Toronto City Hall

Anne Miller

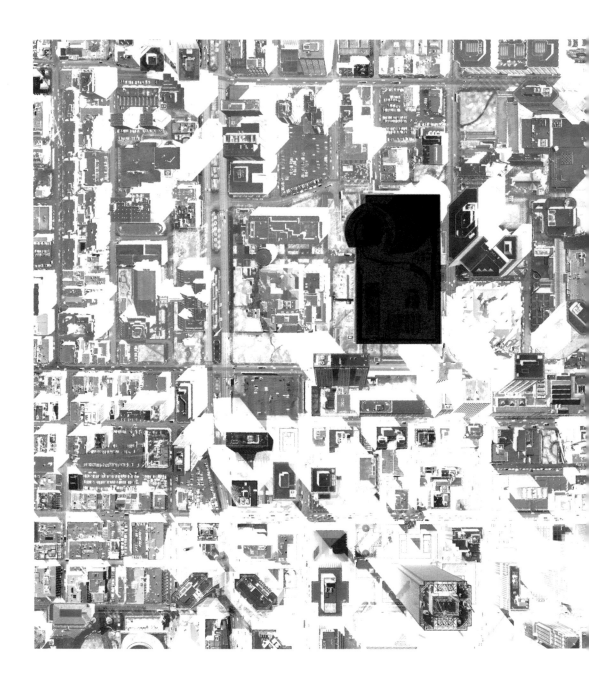

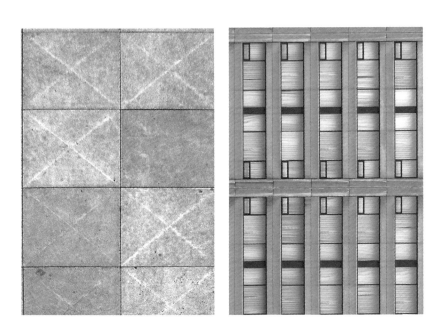

Likely second only to the CN Tower, Viljo Revell's concrete complex is now the most rec-
ognized symbol of Toronto. Miller's photographic abstractions of the Toronto City Hall on
Nathan Phillips Square emphasize the exposed concrete structure as a 'fine grain' gridded
surface at the boomerang shaped towers, and at the concrete pavers that blanket the vast
plaza. Although faceted, at this scale the abstracted surfaces render a smooth sculptural
form, a-particularized and excluding any iconic motifs. It wipes the historic and cultural slate
clean, and exalts concrete, in 1965, to civic status in Toronto.

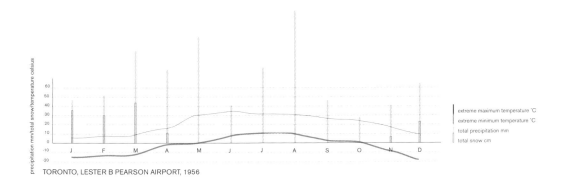

TORONTO, LESTER B PEARSON AIRPORT, 1956

Abstraction of Gardiner
On-Ramp

Eric Van Ziffle

Along eight kilometres of concrete infrastructure, we find a series of unique urban vistas. Van Ziffle's photographic abstractions of the infamous Gardiner Expressway, the City of Toronto's most contentious elevated highway, capture the bleakness of its continuous concrete 'view finder'. Completed in 1964, it is the underside of the Gardiner Expressway that suffers neglect. Travelling parallel to the City's waterfront, it connects the east and west ends, however, the City continues to accuse this obstructing piece of now stained and corroded concrete infrastructure of disconnecting the waterfront from its city.

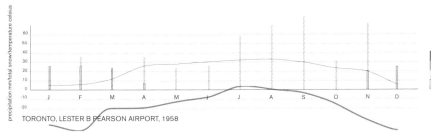

TORONTO, LESTER B PEARSON AIRPORT, 1958

precipitation mm/total snow/temperature celsius

extreme maximum temperature °C
extreme minimum temperature °C
total precipitation mm
total snow cm

Abstraction of
The Larkin Building

Gary Chien

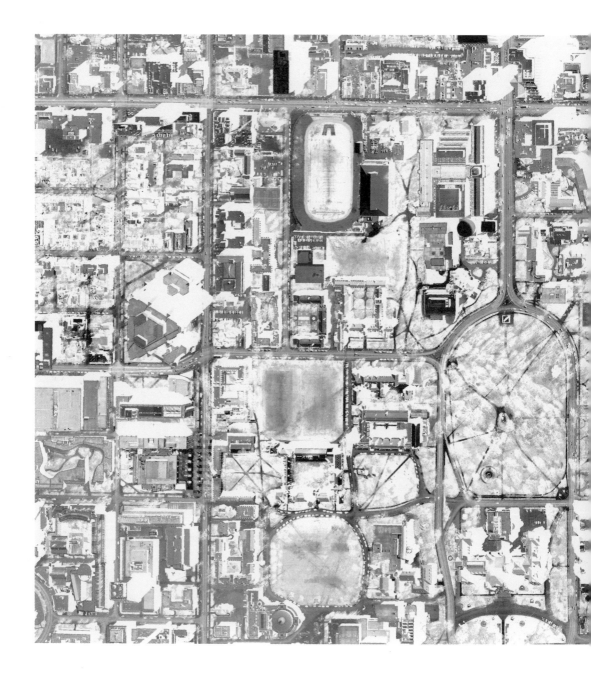

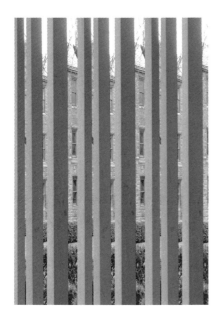

The concrete colonnade sports no bases or capitals. Instead, unadulterated three-storey high columns sit in line in stark contrast to the surrounding 19th century context. Chien's photographic abstractions of the Ontario Institute for Studies in Education on the University of Toronto campus exaggerate the relentless vertical articulation of the thick pilasters and ribbed precast panels that negotiate the interface between the immense precast concrete order, and the rather domesticated scale of existing stone academic buildings. Completed in 1968, like other campus concrete buildings built during this unmatched decade of accelerated growth for the University, OISE was not a well-received addition to the city.

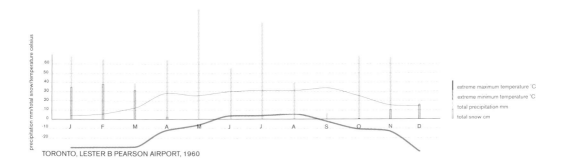

TORONTO, LESTER B PEARSON AIRPORT, 1960

extreme maximum temperature °C
extreme minimum temperature °C
total precipitation mm
total snow cm

Abstraction of Philosopher's Walk

Jessie Grebenc

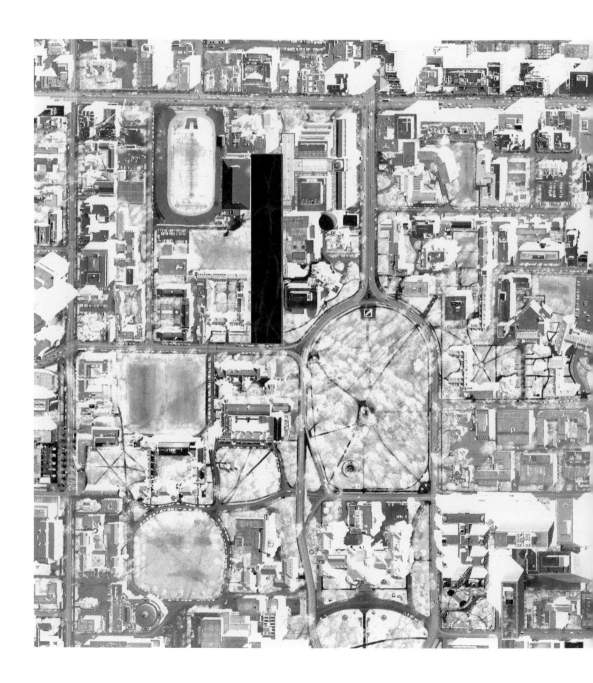

Twenty-four slender concrete columns surround the perimeter of a massive concrete plinth that rises up from the lower valley. Grebenc's abstraction of the edges of the University of Toronto's Edward Johnson Building isolate the evidence of slow scarring by natural elements on the 1961 concrete surface that faces the 'creep' of Philosopher's Walk – a shallow ravine through which Taddle Creek formerly flowed. The strong concrete edge works among many strategies intent on taming the Taddle Creek Ravine and registers passing time and the dramatic climatic swings of freezing and thawing of Canadian cities.

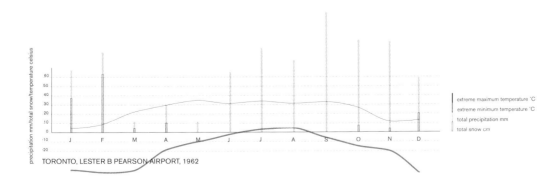

TORONTO, LESTER B PEARSON AIRPORT, 1962

extreme maximum temperature °C
extreme minimum temperature °C
total precipitation mm
total snow cm

Abstraction
of the CN Tower

Shirley Lee

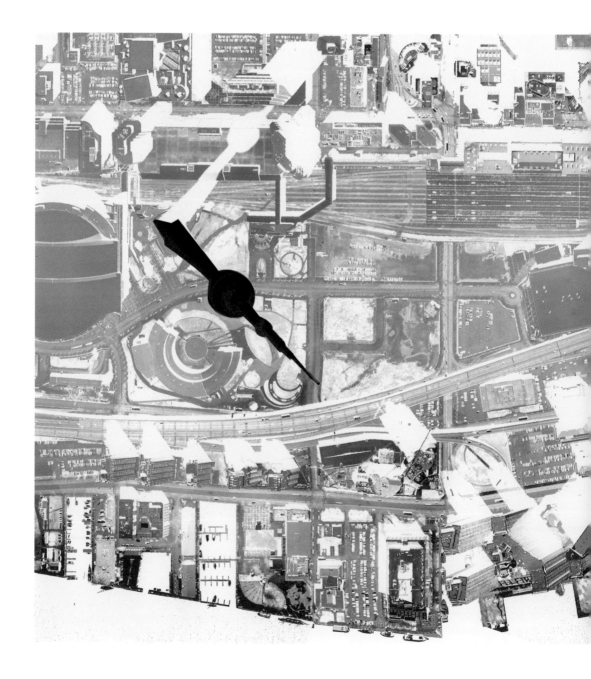

The innovative slip form, that made possible the tallest building in the world, leaves a series of ring-like impressions on the finished surface. Lee's photographic abstraction of the CN Tower, completed in 1976, exaggerates these horizontal markings much like a series of growth rings rising up exactly 553.3 metres above the railway lands. With the CN Tower, concrete stood for an optimism of modernity, and finally achieves monumental status in Toronto. It grows, literally, from the thick striations of railway tracks that strangle its base and hold it at bay from the more accretive, complex city.

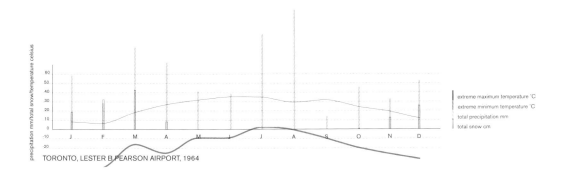

precipitation mm/total snow/temperature celsius

extreme maximum temperature °C
extreme minimum temperature °C
total precipitation mm
total snow cm

TORONTO, LESTER B PEARSON AIRPORT, 1964

Abstraction
of the Medical Sciences
Building

Vanessa Graham

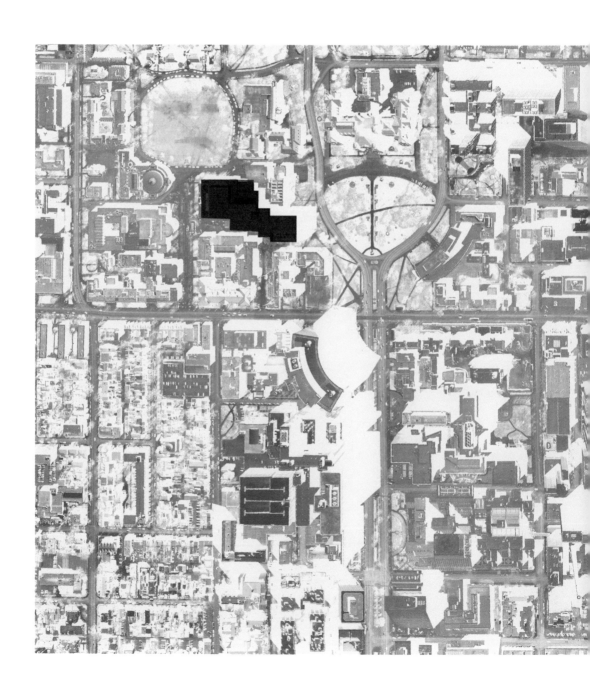

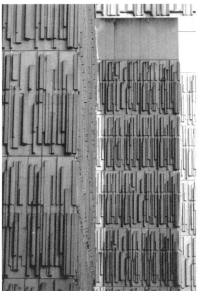

The precast panels of an innovative rain screen wall system sit anything but quietly against the backdrop of the University of Toronto's historic King's College Circle. Graham's photographic abstractions of the Medical Sciences Building bring into focus the seemingly random depths of the unconventionally haptic, sculpted precast panels. The eccentric ribbed panels were (unintentionally) installed randomly giving the façade a seemingly natural rather than machined or engineered aesthetic. Six or seven variations of precast panels in random order articulate the surface of this massive building, giving it a rich, deep texture much like a classical frieze.

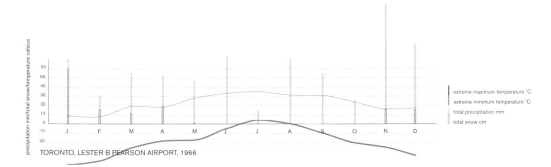

TORONTO, LESTER B PEARSON AIRPORT, 1966

extreme maximum temperature ˚C
extreme minimum temperature ˚C
total precipitation mm
total snow cm

Kenzie Thompson
John P. Robarts Library, Toronto

OPERATION

-noun
'a procedure aimed at restoring or improving the health... such as by correcting a malformation, removing diseased parts, implanting new parts, etc.'

'operation,' definition #10. Dictionary.com, Random House

The most significant transformations in the performance and behaviour of concrete begin at the molecular level. As expounded in the inventory of current concrete technologies in the introduction of this book, new techniques in additives/admixtures combined with new tectonic strategies within refined and inventive formwork can produce a super material unrecognizably related (from a performance point of view) to its brutalist grandparents. The surface features and general appearance, however, tend to maintain an uncanny similarity. As always, exposed concrete surface registers the particulars, perfections, and lack thereof, of its mould.

The otherwise grainless and veinless material takes on the texture of its creator, and often assumes a further enhanced texture via surface treatments that exaggerate and define an otherwise 'blank' face into a requisite sublime abstraction, once the form is long gone. Manual treatments include: embossing, point-tooling, bush hammering, and comb chiseling which works the surface with a bolster chisel to a depth of about 4-5mm.[1] Mechanical treatments include: sawing, splitting, grinding, and polishing, which usually involves a form of fine grinding with paraffins or resins.[2] Finally, technical treatments include: blasting, flaming, and acid etching where the surface of the concrete is washed with diluted acid and water to expose the aggregate.[3]

How can the now most commonplace building material resurface as a critical presence in the city? Can a series of tectonic 'operations' exaggerate, so to speak, the banality of this collection to render and maintain in principle a sublime awesomeness?

1. Bundesverband der Deutschen Zementindustrie, *Concrete Construction Manual* (Basel, Boston, Berlin: Birkhauser, 2002) p.69.
2. ibid p.70
3. ibid pp.72-73

2008

Mark West
Fabric Formwork

a thin formwork membrane contains wet concrete and deflects into precise tension geometries, producing naturally efficient structural curves, unprecedented sculptural forms and delicate surface finishes

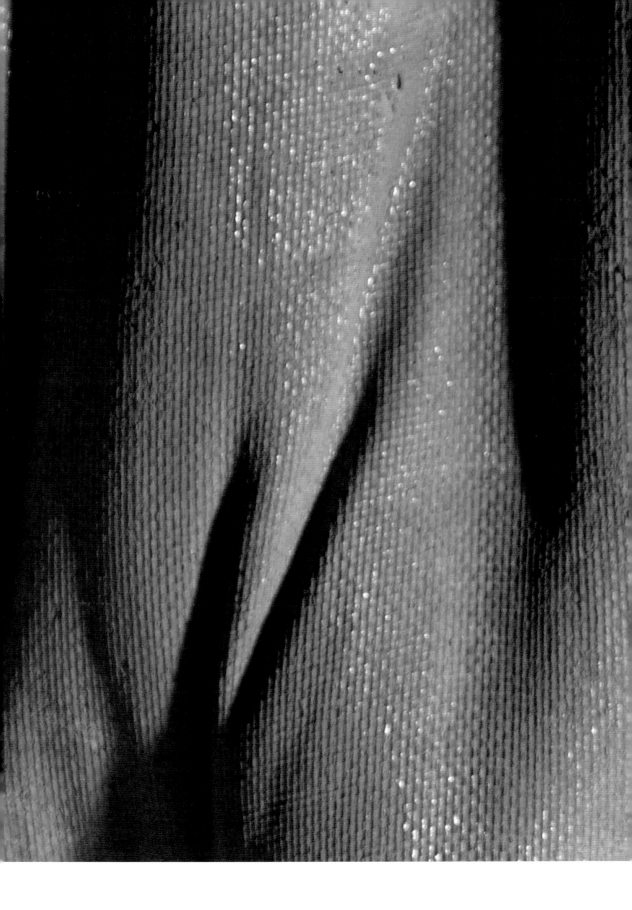

2010   Zaha Hadid
MAXXI

fins of glass-fibre-reinforced concrete emphasize the
curvilinear flow of the galleries

1971   **Ted Bieler**
Helix of Life

a system of precise site-assembled precast concrete
units becomes sculptural art

Chronos Chromos Concrete

Illuminating Concrete

It's just a concept for now, but three designers at the 'Innovation Unit' of the Royal College of Art in London have created a design for concrete that can double as an information display. Called Chronos Chromos Concrete®, it's concrete mixed with thermochromic ink and has nickel chromium wires installed below or behind the concrete surface. When you want to display patterns or information, wires conduct small amounts of heat that induce the thermochromic ink to fluoresce.

"This colouring changing concrete technology was developed through an interest in trying to redefine the most typical characteristics of concrete. When someone builds with concrete they assume that the structure will remain unchanged for years to come. By developing a way to make the concrete surface have a perceivable dynamic character, the material becomes easier for people to relate to."

Afshin Mehin
Innovation Unit, Royal College of Art

Conceptual image showing proposed digital clock concrete wall. Designers are also working on a prototype for a new London train station.

Conductive Concrete

Conductive concrete is produced by adding electrically conductive components to a regular concrete mix to attain stable electrical conductivity. Due to its electrical resistance, a thin layer of conductive concrete can generate enough heat to prevent ice formation on concrete pavement when connected to an AC power source. It is a concrete mix, 1.5 percent of which is steel fibres and 25 percent is steel shavings developed specifically for concrete bridge deck de-icing.

"This project will demonstrate that conductive concrete technology has national and international importance. Statistics indicate that 10% to 15% of all roadway accidents are directly related to weather conditions. This percentage alone represents thousands of human injuries and deaths and millions of dollars in property damage annually. The payoff potential is tremendous. This revolutionary deicing technology is applicable to accident-prone areas such as bridge overpasses, exit ramps, airport runways, street intersections, sidewalks, and driveways."

Christopher Y. Tuan, *Ph.D., P.E., Associate Professor of Civil Engineering, University of Nebraska*

Synthetic nanocrystalline iron oxide particles.

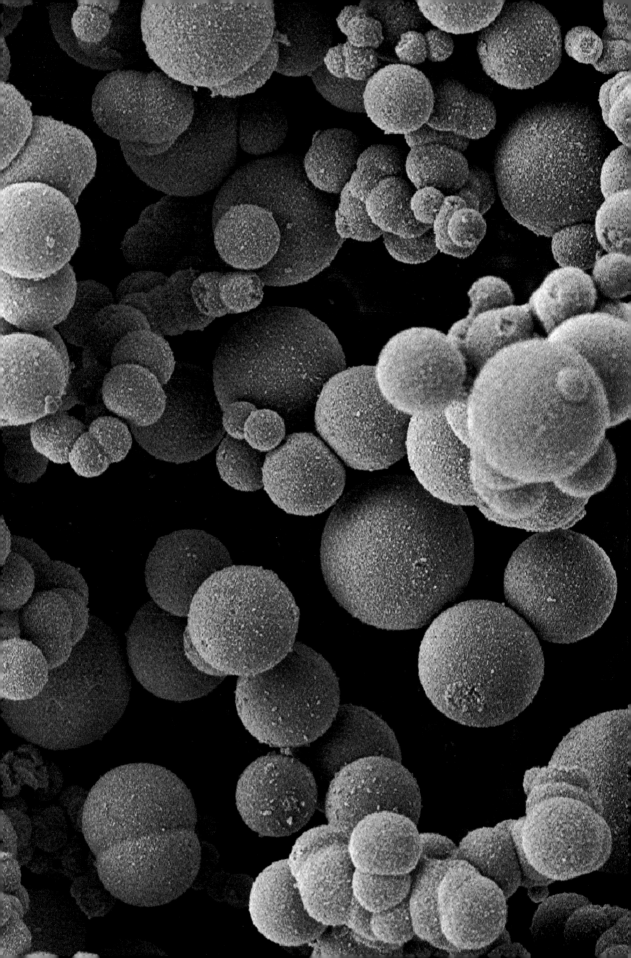

Creacrete™
ceramic concrete

Creacrete™ is a concrete based material which is highly dense and compact, making it possible to create filigree and thin-walled objects out of concrete. Special processing makes it possible to achieve a durable glossy surface which is new to concrete. A nano-scale coating makes cups and plates hydrophobic and food-safe. Creacrete™ uses an energy-saving cold-casting process, and is an alternative to ceramics for floor and wall coverings, decorative objects and façades.

"The function of the product determines the process... I work in a cultural context but my work is multi-disciplinary... Some of the pieces are very arty and some are influenced by material sciences."

Creacrete inventor and designer
Alexa Lixfeld as quoted in **Wallpaper**
December issue 2008

Creacrete™ detail.

concrete climate

Sarah Iwata

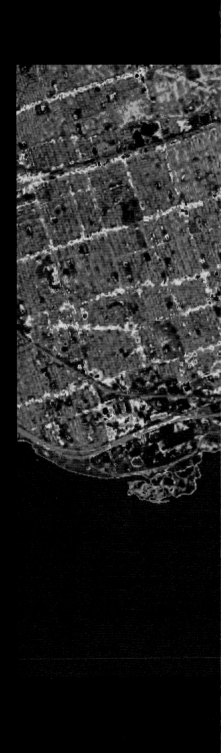

Snaking westbound along Toronto's Gardiner Expressway as it hugs the Don River's course to Lake Ontario, the highway allows the city skyline, punctuated by the CN Tower, to reveal itself cinematographically above the tree line. The monumental magic of the modern city is encapsulated in this scene – constantly replayed every trip at 100km/Hr through the windshield of a car. Turning to travel along the lake, the Gardiner lifts above the industrial flats and defunct shipping lanes allowing views through the city towers and drifting daringly close to the massive base of the CN Tower. Despite this poetic vision, the raised roadway has been accused of severing the city from its natural lake front. The industrial rail yards, industrial brown fields, and largely abandoned shipping lanes south of the Gardiner have yet to be redeveloped for commercial or residential use. In the interim, massive swathes of unsightly surface parking levelled on old dockyards seem to be the only viable use for the area.

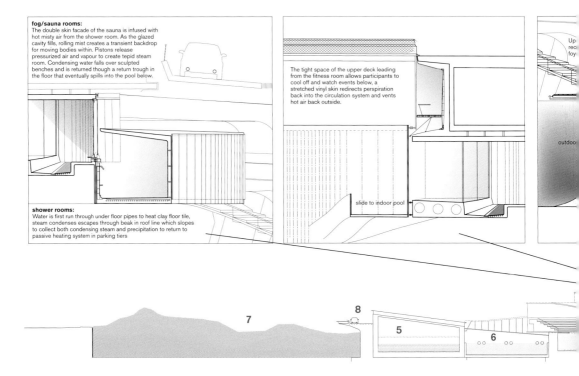

fog/sauna rooms:
The double skin facade of the sauna is infused with hot misty air from the shower room. As the glazed cavity fills, rolling mist creates a transient backdrop for moving bodies within. Pistons release pressurized air and vapour to create tepid steam room. Condensing water falls over sculpted benches and is returned though a return trough in the floor that eventually spills into the pool below.

The tight space of the upper deck leading from the fitness room allows participants to cool off and watch events below, a stretched vinyl skin redirects perspiration back into the circulation system and vents hot air back outside.

Up
rec
foy

outdoo

slide to indoor pool

shower rooms:
Water is first run through under floor pipes to heat clay floor tile, steam condenses escapes through beak in roof line which slopes to collect both condensing steam and precipitation to return to passive heating system in parking tiers

7

8

5

6

1. outdoor leisure pool
2. 25m indoor pool and grandstand
3. change rooms
4. parking pad
5. cistern
6. pond for recreational canoeing
7. retention pond
8. automobile circulation ramp

North of the Gardiner, Front Street provides the new boundary condition to the city, allowing the massive stone façade of Union Station, the city's passenger train station, to anchor the downtown grid and turn its back to the lake. With its massive concrete underbelly and monumental piers, the Gardiner has done much to consolidate a negative image of concrete in the collective cultural psyche of Toronto. Completed in 1966, the controversy today centres around when, rather than if, the monumental piece of modernist infrastructure should be torn down and remade into a wide boulevard to reconnect Toronto's citizens with their long forgotten lake.[1]

Unfortunately, this optimistic plan for 'undoing' fails to renegotiate the relationship of the city with the automobile. Diversion of traffic underground or along surface routes and the relocation of parking spaces present new challenges to the revitalization plan. In addition, the historic docks-cum-parking lots have sculpted a shoreline evocative of a toothy grin, devoid of graded beach or gentle curve. Given these conditions, it is difficult to imagine how the mere removal of a vital city artery would result in such an idyllic transformation. If the Gardiner was a mistake its effects are not so easily erased.

Perhaps it is possible to exchange our aversion for appreciation and play with the cards we have been dealt. How might we make the functional and infrastructural, monumental and experiential; and reaffirm, rather than remake, our relation to the lake? A positive concrete identity may only be a matter of perception.

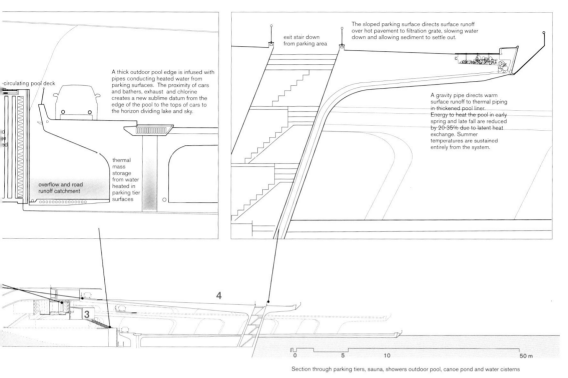

A thick outdoor pool edge is infused with pipes conducting heated water from parking surfaces. The proximity of cars and bathers, exhaust and chlorine creates a new sublime datum from the edge of the pool to the tops of cars to the horizon dividing lake and sky.

-circulating pool deck

thermal mass storage from water heated in parking tier surfaces

overflow and road runoff catchment

exit stair down from parking area

The sloped parking surface directs surface runoff over hot pavement to filtration grate, slowing water down and allowing sediment to settle out.

A gravity pipe directs warm surface runoff to thermal piping in thickened pool liner. Energy to heat the pool in early spring and late fall are reduced by 20-35% due to latent heat exchange. Summer temperatures are sustained entirely from the system.

Section through parking tiers, sauna, showers outdoor pool, canoe pond and water cisterns

Figure 2: Longitudinal North-South Section with speculative details enlarged above.

The city burns. Literally.

Constructed from asphalt, brick, and concrete, the urban material palette attracts, retains and re-radiates the sun's energy enough to amplify local temperatures; in contrast to the moderating cool body of the lake. Using data collected through satellite imagery, the albedo effect is a startling painted technicolour map of the urban microclimate. Dark coloured materials which absorb UV radiation can account for 33% of the ambient temperature in an urban area[2]. In addition, scientists have found that at times when the air temperature might be 80 degrees Fahrenheit, the material surface temperatures of the city were 120 degrees. Such extreme temperatures can have surprising effects, even generating unique weather or increasing urban smog levels[3]. Viewed in this way, concrete's cold grey pallor and stoic presence becomes something mutable, fleshy, alive and at times dangerously hot. The recoloured map of Toronto (see Figure 1) allows boundaries between infrastructure and building, surfaces and objects to dissolve – allowing the presence of one body to be felt by another. Like temperature, other weather effects such as wind vectors (speed and direction), seasonal lake levels, humidity and precipitation generate a unique micro-climatic condition that the built environment both influences and responds to. Temperature differences between surface and air allow particles of water to move at different speeds, slowing to condense as droplets on glass or quickening and escaping as vaporous gas. Changes in the physical state of water and the thermal properties of concrete allow for phenomenological effects to occur – transforming the mundane into the fantastic.

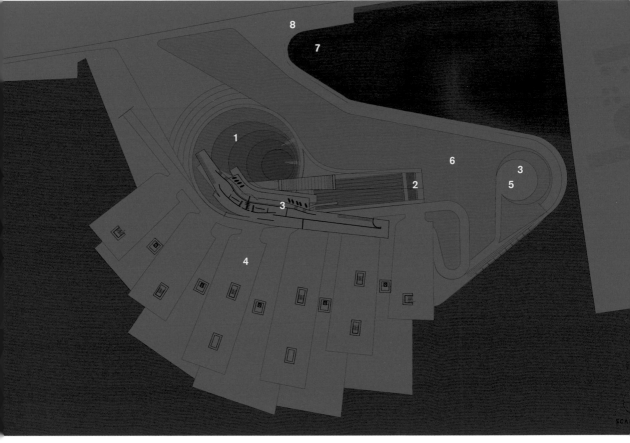

Figure 3: Level 4 Plan.
1. beach entry outdoor leisure pool
2. 25 m indoor lap pool and grandstand
3. change rooms
4. parking pad

5. cistern
6. overflow pond for recreational canoeing
7. retention ponds to control outflow to lake
8. parking entrance

Figure 4: View of beach entry to public pool with layered change, sauna and shower facilities in the background.

Figure 5: View from bottom tier of parking showing layered concrete pads and piers above. Full of cars, the parking lot becomes the characteristic foreground to the lake views.

390 cubic metres of annual precipitation falls on the prescribed parking surface and is collected into subsurface piping.

And yet, these very effects are what traditional notions of building envelope are meant to prevent. Sealants, air and water barriers, flashing and insulation seek to provide a hermetic separation between the interior and exterior elements. In addition, to procure a perfect indoor air temperature, great mechanical effort is required. As a result, the conversation between interior and exterior is highly controlled and tightly constrained within a narrowly prescribed 'comfort zone'.

But what if we allow weather, and its intrinsic unpredictability, in?

The project presented here allows for a new space in between interior and exterior. By exploring the potential microclimate created by concrete and water to moderate air quality, a series of controlled and uncontrolled spaces are proposed. Using a waterfront site at the base of the main North-South Toronto thoroughfare, an existing, 700 car, surface parking lot is feathered and strategically heaped to one side to accommodate a large circular public pool. As a 'smog-eating' TX Active coated concrete wind barrier, the site becomes both heroic infrastructure and recreational landscape in a vernacular not so foreign to the surrounding context (see Figure 3).

Rather than prevent the creep of water into a conditioned interior, speculative details (see Figure 2) control its entry, direct its path and exploit its ability to carry and move heat. The transmutable character of water becomes a transient surface effect mitigated by momentary variables of heat, prevalent wind conditions and automobile occupation. Intimate and bodily delights become the fantastic result of asphalt sprawl. Here, concrete is employed for both its traditional visual aesthetic, and its ability to retain and distribute energy.

The new CarPool occupies a tenuous position which accepts and celebrates both urban and natural effects of atmosphere in a decidedly sublime search for new modes of public experience, views, and ideologies of waterfront revitalization through parking infrastructure (see conceptual renderings Figures 4, 5, 6, 7). Concrete works.

390 cubic metres of annual precipitation falls on the prescribed parking surface and is collected into subsurface piping. Convection allows the circulating water to pick up latent heat from the parking surface and distribute it around the thick insulating concrete liner of the 50 metre circular outdoor swimming pool. Excess water is released into a series of carved pools that both treat and cool the water. Treated water is reserved in a large cistern and used to flood the inner marsh creating an even surface of ice for winter skating (refer to section details in Figure 2 and plan in Figure 3).

Formally derived in response to localized wind vectors, turning radii and the movement of liquids over curved surfaces, the project is challenged to reconcile diverse programs of swimming, driving, sweating, idling and diving. As a result, the forced and perhaps sometimes perverse juxtaposition of program, further mitigated by the unpredictable influence of weather events, creates a sensorial experience not normally appreciated or forecasted.

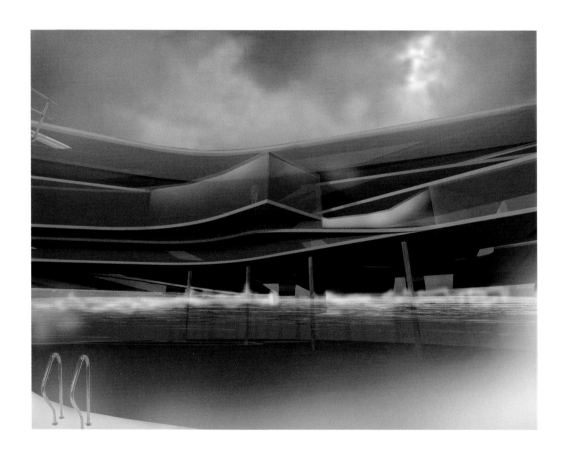

Figure 6: Conceptual rendering of the parking structure from
the outdoor pool as it foregrounds the view to the lake.

Figure 7: Conceptual rendering of the
upper level parking structure.

Rendered as something atmospheric and an active participant in a constantly shifting microclimate, the CarPool project simultaneously celebrates and challenges previously held notions of concrete materiality. Fashioned into heroic concrete piers and parking pads the project is both a reference to the city's historical highway building, as well as a vision of a future where concrete, through its material and visceral properties, redefines our urban experience. Re-engineered, the CarPool's use of concrete as an active, contemporary material, reframes our response to its established cultural status.

1. As the on-ramp to an expressway that was never built, the Gardiner Expressway east was built with the intention of creating a new highway connection with south Scarborough, an eastern Toronto suburb. Growing construction costs and public outcry resulted in only a short 1.3 kilometre section of the planned connection ever being built. Citing prohibitive maintenance expenses, Toronto City Council voted to remove this appendage as the first section of the Gardiner to be demolished in 1999. Recently, in May of 2008, Mayor David Miller backed a $300 million plan to remove the Gardiner Expressway east of Jarvis Street and transform it into an eight-lane, at-grade roadway in eight years. Less ambitious than the $1.8 billion 2006 proposal to level the entire elevated portion of the highway, the mayor has decided that "the potential for taking down other parts of the Gardiner is a discussion for the next generation". Mayor David Miller, May 30, 2008, David Nickle, *The Scarborough Mirror* http://www.insidetoronto.ca/News/Scarborough/article/49178

2. "White Roofs Could Reduce Urban Heat Island Effect By 33 Percent" Keith Oleson, National Center for Atmospheric Research (NCAR) Geophysical Research Letters in press as reported by *Science 2.0* http://www.science20.com/news_articles/white_roofs_could_reduce_urban_heat_island_effect_33_percent

3. The urban heat island effect as described by Dale Quattrochi, senior researcher at the Global Hydrology and Climate Center, part of NASA's Marshall Space Flight Center in Huntsville, Alabama, in *Science Central*, "Heat Islands", by Jill Max, July 9, 2000: http://www.sciencentral.com/articles/view.php3?article_id=218391191

Figure 8. Acrylic physical model 1:250 scale

Petrzalka, Moscow

operation

Tower Hamlets, London

operation

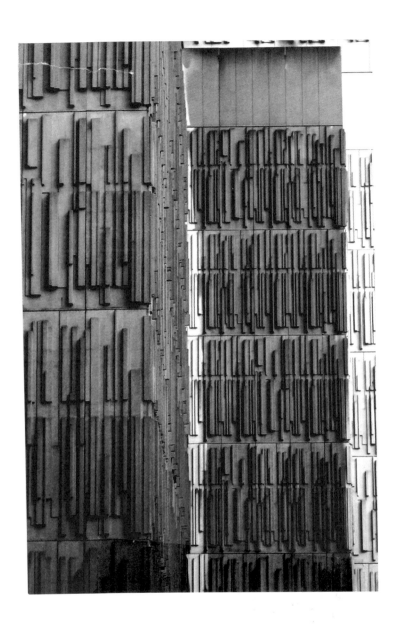

Vanessa Graham
Abstraction of Medical Sciences Building

notes on operation

Today, the city of Toronto, whose vast climatic range is challenged perhaps only by the Canadian prairie cities of Winnipeg and Edmonton, boasts one of the greatest collections of 50s, 60s and 70s concrete buildings. The city's consuming grey sky might have a dimming effect on these shining moments in concrete; however, it allows us to isolate then transform, therefore, the devices that arm the existing robust collection of concrete stock with sufficient degrees of brutal abstraction, in order to anticipate and speculate on their new presence in the city.

Operation: Weaving of Sheraton Centre

Alessia Soppelsa

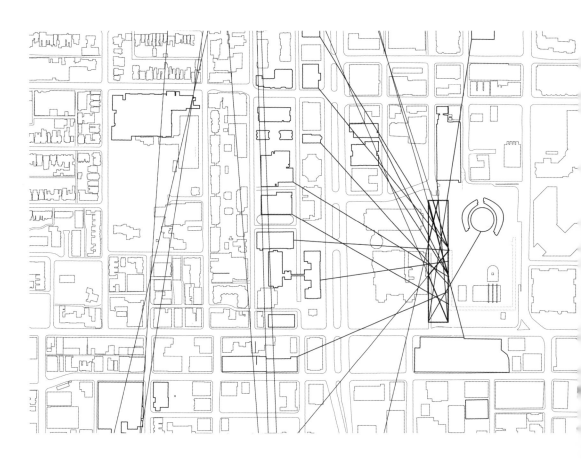

Operation: Weaving

The tried and true 'broken-rib precast panel', known for its efficient water-shedding capacity while defying its machined aesthetic, is challenged.

Weaving interlaces the concrete bands of the Sheraton Centre's broken-rib panel imperfectly, as if fashioned by hand. It visually interprets the rain-screen wall as a water repellent textile, and makes the matt-like texture hyper.

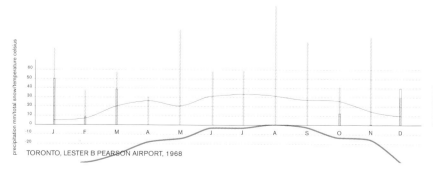

extreme maximum temperature °C
extreme minimum temperature °C
total precipitation mm
total snow cm

TORONTO, LESTER B PEARSON AIRPORT, 1968

Operation: Snagging of Toronto City Hall

Anne Miller

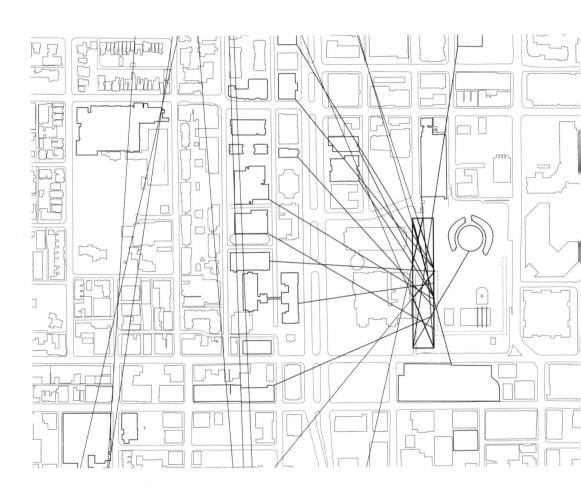

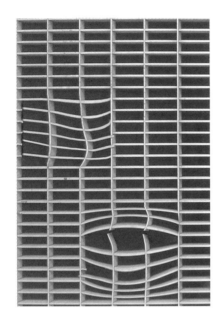

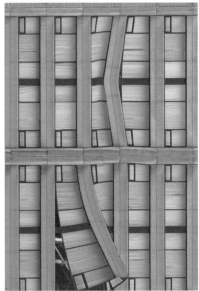

Operation: Snagging

The grid seems to find its way into and onto the modern surface for its de-particularizing effects. Snagging interprets the surface grid as having thickness. It renders a kind of textile whose seams or stitches can stretch disproportionately to interrupt the homogeneous surface, and create particularizing features where there were none before. Like a snag in a stocking that breaks the taut hold of the skin it envelopes.

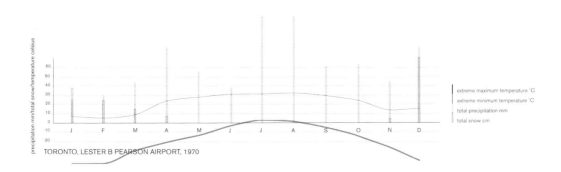

TORONTO, LESTER B PEARSON AIRPORT, 1970

extreme maximum temperature °C
extreme minimum temperature °C
total precipitation mm
total snow cm

Operation: Corroding Gardiner Expressway On-Ramp

Eric Van Ziffle

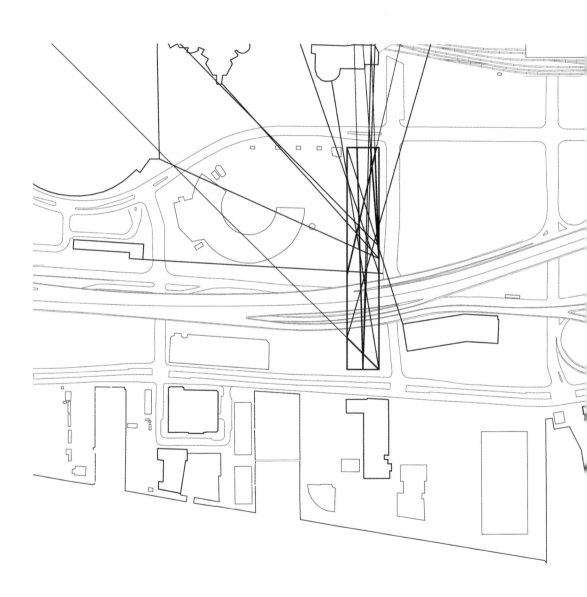

Operation: Corroding

Steel reinforcing has allowed seemingly infinite structural possibilities in concrete. Robust, grand large-scale infrastructures bisect the city with no embellishment.

Corroding looks at the potential of wilful eroding of the robust, plumb Gardiner Expressway to exaggerate sublime aspects of its city-framing underside. Previously obstructed views are now 'leaking-in' and new oblique connections are made with the ascending off-ramp structure.

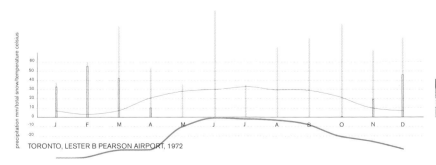

extreme maximum temperature °C
extreme minimum temperature °C
total precipitation mm
total snow cm

TORONTO, LESTER B PEARSON AIRPORT, 1972

Operation: Repetition of the Larkin Building

Gary Chein

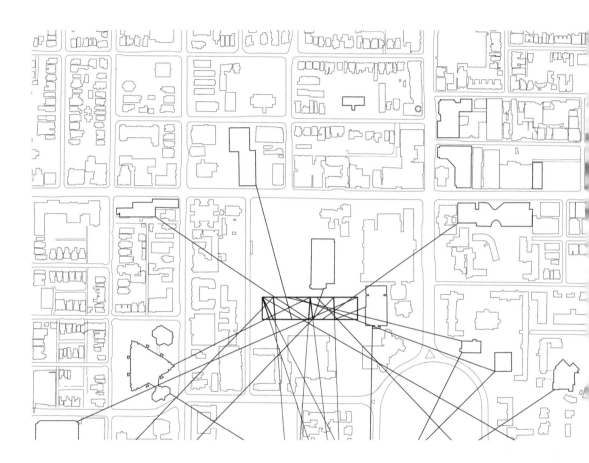

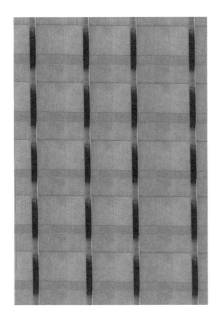
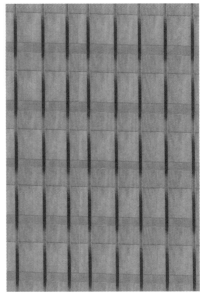

Operation: Repetition

Repeated elements in brutalism, like the grid, afford a kind of a-particularized self-referential 'field' – an abstracted surface that wipes the cultural slate clean, so to speak.

Repeating exaggerates the engineered, relentless concrete brutalist elements to make the centreless, featureless, and minimalist surface hyper to the point of a dizzying disorientation. The stripped colonnade becomes transporting, and the neo-gothic adjacent context is equally broken into unrecognizable shards.

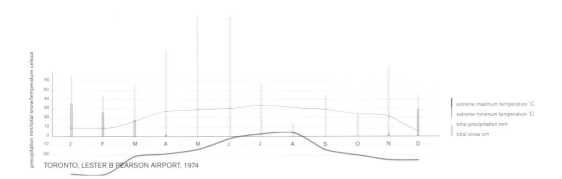

TORONTO, LESTER B PEARSON AIRPORT, 1974

Operation: Scarring of Philosopher's Walk

Jessie Grebenc

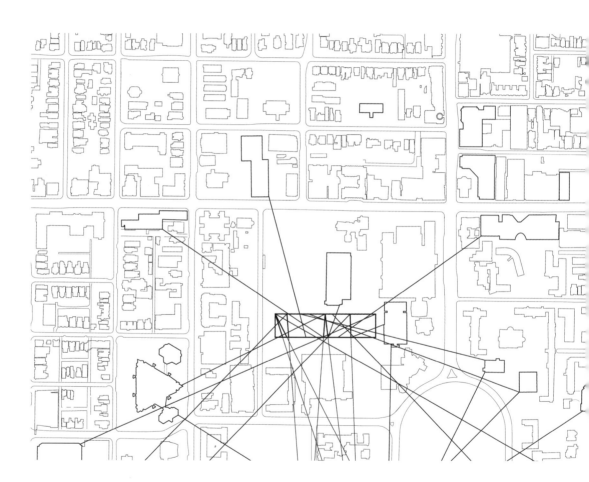

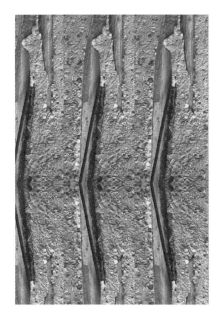
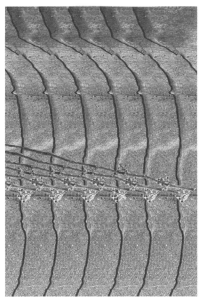

Operation: Scarring

There are few building materials that protect us from fire and noise like massive, dense concrete. It is all-powerful and very low-maintenance, however, it is subject to deterioration by the elements.

Scarring interrupts the consistency of the perfectly smooth concrete surface by strategically 'injuring' its surface to create a marked, modelled pattern. The engineered surface is now afflicted by cracks and wrinkles. It succumbs to a kind of grain or veining akin to a natural, as-found material.

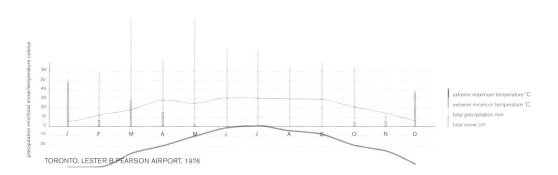

TORONTO, LESTER B PEARSON AIRPORT, 1976

extreme maximum temperature °C
extreme minimum temperature °C
total precipitation mm
total snow cm

Operation: Threading of the CN Tower

Shirley Lee

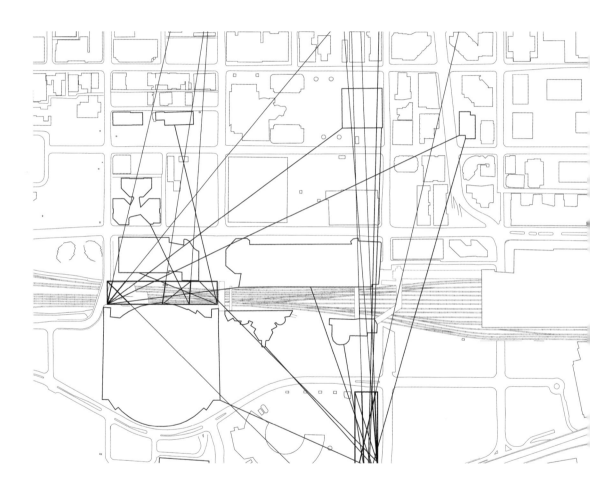

Operation: Threading

Béton Brut promises a kind of honest nudity that reflects a no-nonsense, forward-looking aesthetic. Every nuance of the inner mould is imprinted on its formed surface, and a slipping or 'flying' form will register the horizontal start and stop of each consecutive pour. Threading compresses these resulting 'growth rings' to create a new density of horizontal lines that exaggerate its scale and so render the already tall structure with a more sublime awesomeness.

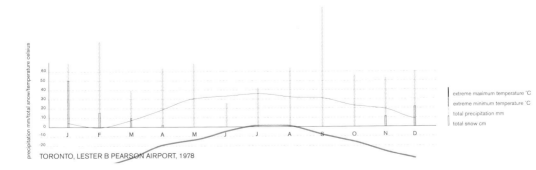

TORONTO, LESTER B PEARSON AIRPORT, 1978

extreme maximum temperature °C
extreme minimum temperature °C
total precipitation mm
total snow cm

Operation: Delaminating of the Medical Sciences Building

Vanessa Graham

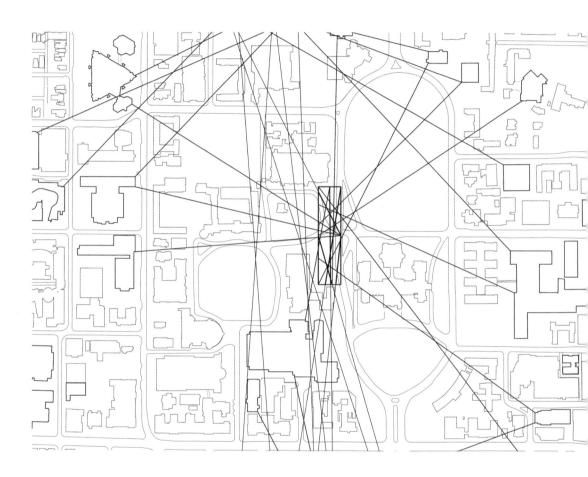

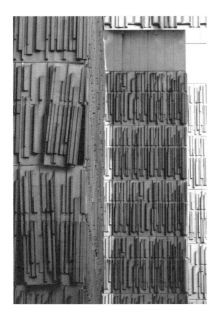

Operation: Delaminating

In 1961, the rain-screen wall system was quite new. In this system lightweight panels and joints deflect most of the water and the ventilated cavity eliminates the remaining moisture through natural drainage and evaporation.

Delaminating splits and dislodges the sculpted concrete precast panels by obstructing the necessary cavity. Water pressure rises and at moments of weakness, the taut face of concrete breaks and perfectly square panels begin to collide.

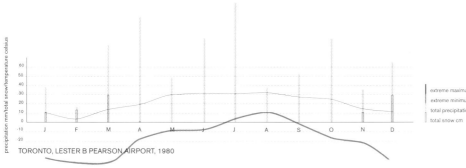

precipitation mm/total snow/temperature celsius

extreme maximum temperature °C
extreme minimum temperature °C
total precipitation mm
total snow cm

TORONTO, LESTER B PEARSON AIRPORT, 1980

Alessia Soppelsa
Abstraction of Sheraton Centre

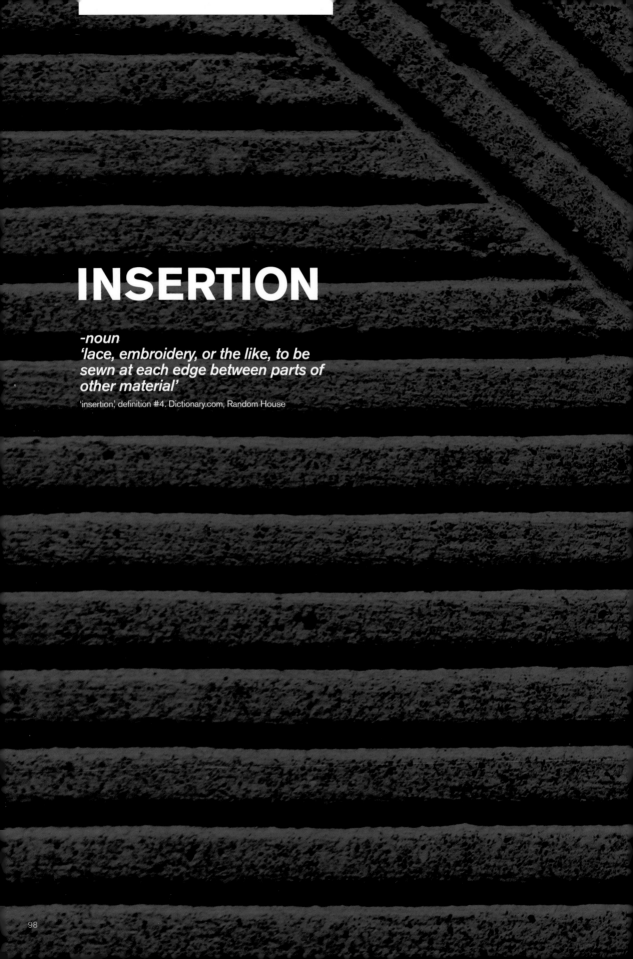

INSERTION

-noun
'lace, embroidery, or the like, to be
sewn at each edge between parts of
other material'

'insertion,' definition #4. Dictionary.com, Random House

In the introduction to her anthology *Concrete Design*, Sarah Gaventa explains how 'concrete' is considered a dirty word, synonymous with 'shoddy', 'cheap', and even 'inhuman' by the vast majority of the public.[1] Despite the increasing number of spectacular works of sculptural concrete buildings in recent history, there still exists a general opinion that concrete leads to insensitive buildings. After 50 years, concrete brutalism might begin to acquire appreciation for its vintage value (perhaps mostly by architects and designers); however it is safe to say that some of the worst concrete 'sins' were committed in that time, and must now be corrected. The awesome artistry of the 'unadulterated' abstracted concrete surface of this time still carries this association. The idea that the now 'super' exposed concrete surface can be a site for new artistic production ultimately promises a shift in meaning.

Concrete speaks to the way it's made, and exposed concrete today has not yet significantly changed the persistent language of making the invisible visible – to lay the structure of the building (and its inseparable connection to form and surface) open to the view of the observer/user.

When this structure performs in a way that defies the understood burdens of concrete in compression, then we begin to perceive it differently, even though it might appear, 'on the surface' or 'to the naked eye' more or less as it always has.

We must ask then, whether new surgical concrete interventions in cities rich with 'vintage layers' of concrete fabric, can inevitably begin to define the lens through which existing stock is perceived and ultimately give new meaning to old stigmas.

1. Sarah Gaventa, *Concrete Design* (Great Britain: Mitchell Beazley Publishing, 2001) p.8

2005   **Laurent Savioz**   a lining of insulating concrete (expanded glass) doubles
                        Chamoson House,   as a layer of thermal protection and as support structure,
                        Switzerland   strengthening the existing stone walls of the original
                                                  1814 house

2005

Tadao Ando
*Concrete Cube at the
Palazzo Grassi, Venice*

self-levelling concrete is carefully poured to create a
smooth and polished cube rising vertically within the
volume of the imperfect existing vintage building

2010

Zaha Hadid
MAXXI, Rome

cast on-site in self-compacting concrete with customized
aggregate and admixtures to achieve continuous 50m
long spans

Ductal™
ultra thin concrete

At up to ten times the strength of conventional concrete, Ductal™ developed by Lafarge© and named for its ductile qualities, is more in a class with steel. With reinforcing microfibres, it has up to 30,000 psi of compressive strength rather than the 7000 psi or less of standard concrete. The outstanding strength-to-weight characteristic means that it can be sliced sliver-thin and still hold up.

"Producing Ductal™ requires on average three times less energy than that required to produce a ton of conventional concrete. Furthermore, over its extrapolated field tested life span of 1000 years, the material savings that it enables (between three and six times less than conventional concrete) and the virtual lack of maintenance required can reduce the environmental impact of Ductal™ structures by more than 30% compared with equivalent structures made out of conventional materials."

Jean-Francois Batoz
Director of Development for Ductal™

3cm thick Ductal Concrete panels at the Thiais RATP Bus Depot by ECDM in France.

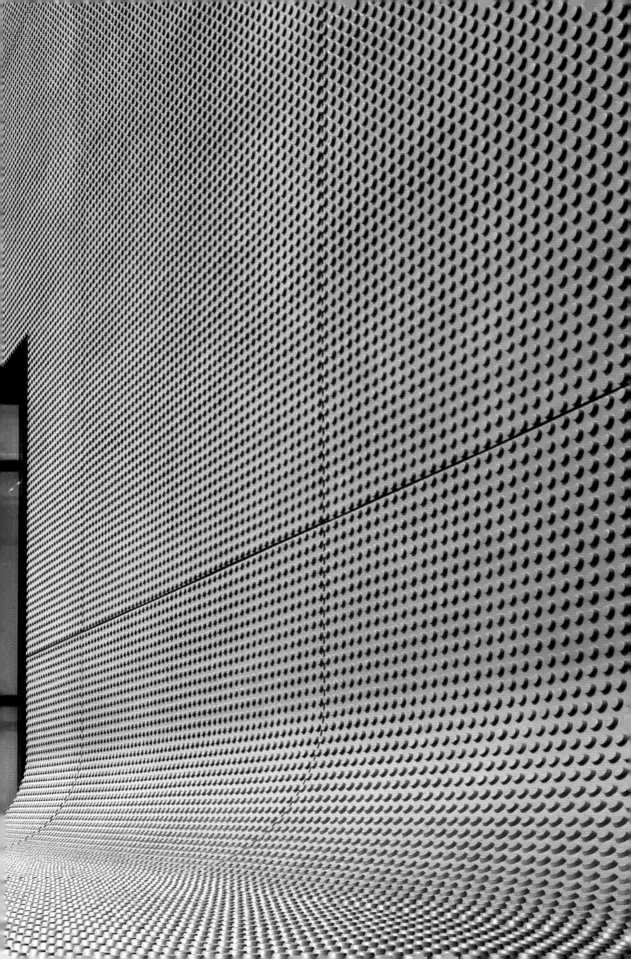

Flowstone
ultra smooth concrete

Flowstone® grey, white and super white are high performance cementitious binders made from Portland Cement and a microfine cement. The production of the concrete can be processed as fluid or self-compacting concrete. For the various applications, Dyckerhoff Flowstone will be supplemented by appropriate aggregates, pigments and additives from the end-user. Flowstone® can have a w/c ratio between 0.29 and 0.35 to achieve a flexure tensile strength up to 15 MPa and a compressive strength of more than 100 MPa and a surface so perfect it approaches the uniformity of plastic.

"For various applications, Dyckerhoff Flowstone is supplemented by appropriate aggregates, pigments and additives from the end-user. Through the wide range of aggregates, fine grained concretes can be realized. Therefore, concrete can be manufactured in different grain sizes and with outstanding, intense colours. Independent of the grain size chosen, the concrete properties will always achieve the strength and durability required."

Product Information brochure
Dyckerhoff Weisszement

Complex voronoid forms are possible through the use of Flowstone® additives.

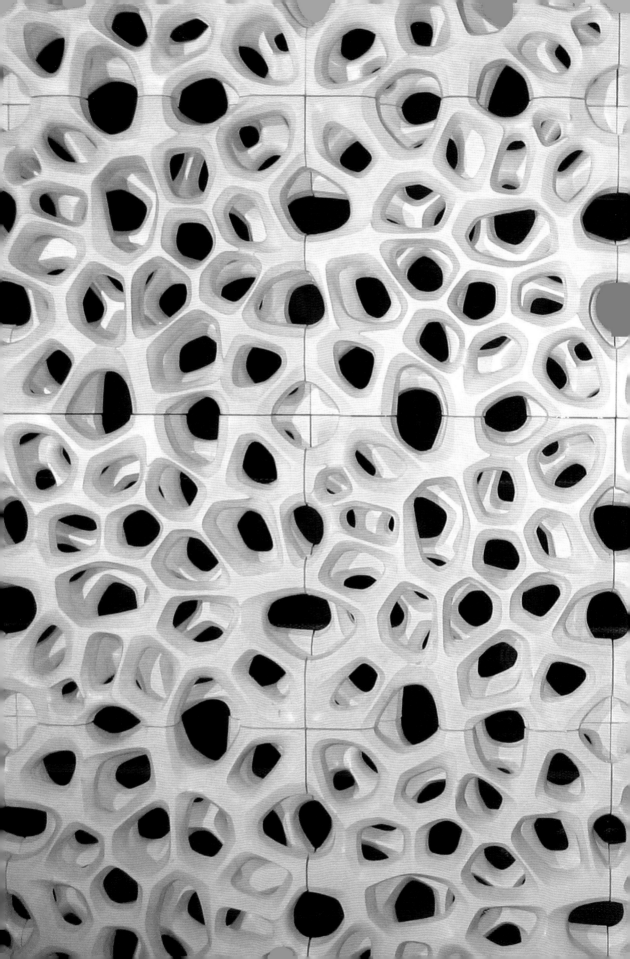

Graphic Concrete™
peri photo engraving

Combining silk-screening and photo engraving techniques it is now possible to etch images onto the face of concrete slabs and precast blocks. Using an image engraved onto a sheet of polystyrene, a chemical additive is applied to the surface as a retarder. The retarder keeps the concrete in contact with the sheet from hardening. Embedded in the mould, the concrete is cast over the sheet. Once it has set for 24 hours the mould and sheet are removed and a pressurized hose removes the concrete from the image area, resulting in the photographic image in relief.

"Graphic Concrete technology enables the manufacturing of unique industrial products that meet the challenges of modern architecture. It thus brings new opportunities both in business and environmental planning. Graphic Concrete is a tool for designing and creating a better and more interesting environment."

Graphic Concrete™ is based on a patented invention by interior architect **Samuli Naamanka**

View of photo-engraved surface relief.

Kenzie Thompson
Abstraction of Queen's Park

notes on insertion

Tracing the distribution of prominent concrete structures across the City of Toronto, the studio examined this collection with fresh eyes. An area of natural concentration, along the ceremonial University Avenue 'spine', became the testing ground for speculations on how a building material such as concrete could be an urban catalyst with a reconsidered aesthetic articulation – one that acknowledges the cultural shifts arguably imposed by current nano material technologies.

Concrete-Dense
City Swathe

threading
filtering

corroding
filtering

snagging
weaving

This concrete-dense city swathe that spans from Toronto's Bloor Street to the north to the edge of Lake Ontario to the south to Spadina Avenue to the west and Yonge Street to the east, provides six strategic sites where we find opportunities to create new urban links in and around some of our often forgotten Toronto concrete treasures. Each site has proximate as well as less proximate relationships to existing concrete structures, which create an unavoidable 'dialogue' while new connections are forged within the morphology of the city. We asked whether new surgical concrete interventions on these sites, only in concert, together create a collective

city museum – one which defines the lens through which its subject of display is perceived.

There exists an unusual flatness to this part of the city. The current lake edge has receded both naturally and, for a small distance, artificially so that the densest inhabitation of the city occurs on the dried bed of ancient Lake Iroquois. The typically Canadian abundance of space here contributed to those factors, which rendered a building material such as concrete, usually reserved for more Mediterranean climates, economical and desirable.

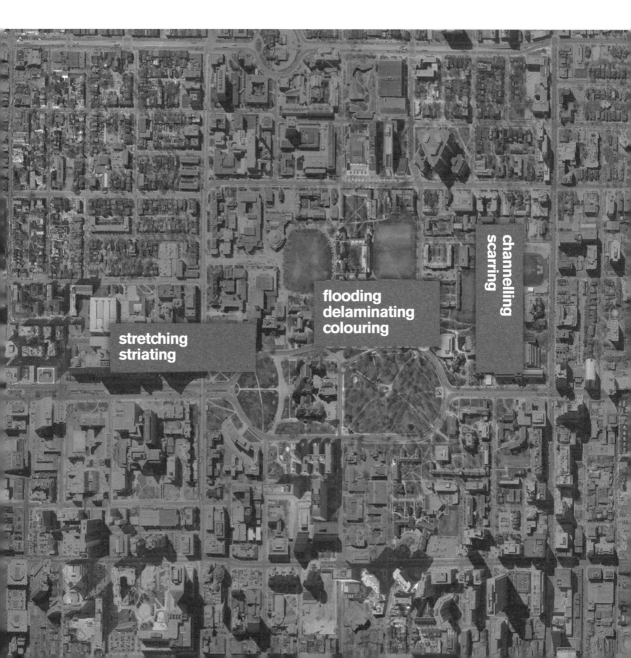

channelling
scarring

flooding
delaminating
colouring

stretching
striating

corroding + filleting + snagging + stretching + delaminating + channelling

One of ninety-six combinations for City Museum

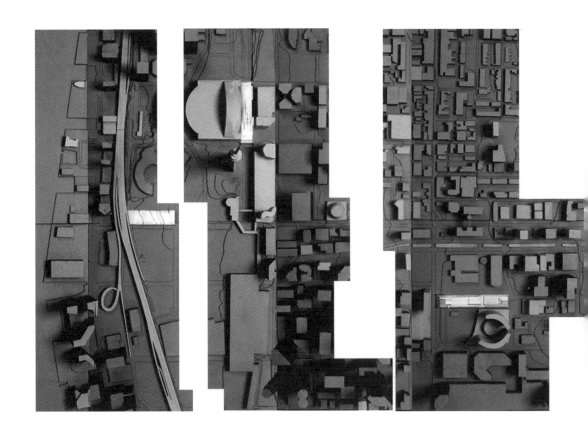

GE: E. VanZiffle
Gardin Fronts

RY: T. Genshorek
Sky Beach

CH: A. Miller
Formal Glitches

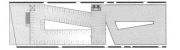

The Gardiner Expressway site (GE) is in the shadow of Toronto's CN Tower completed in 1976 and engulfs the 1964 raised expressway. The GE site can reconnect the city to its lake edge by bridging this concrete obstacle, and reimagining the derelict underbelly of the sublime structure at this strategic moment of what is currently a psychological impasse.

THIS COMBINATION: E. Van Ziffle's 'corroding' Gardin Fronts; T. Genshorek's 'filleting' Sky Beach; A. Miller's 'snagging' Formal Glitches; L. Woofter's 'stretching' Seventh Floor Ground; V. Graham's 'delaminating' Masked; G. Chien's 'channelling' Moving Pictures

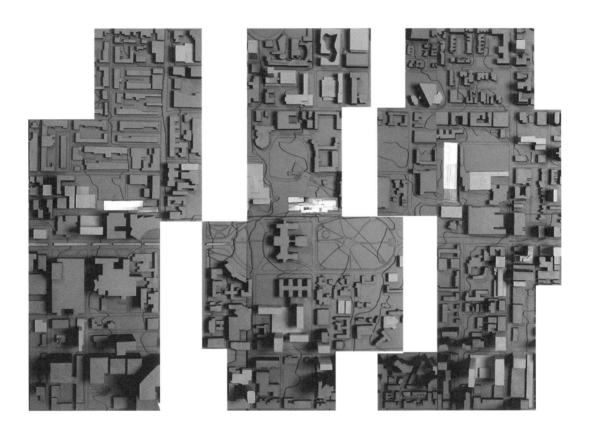

HB: L. Woofter
Seventh Floor Ground

QP: V. Graham
Masked

PW: G. Chien
Moving Pictures

filtering + threading + weaving + striating + flooding + scarring

One of ninety-six combinations for City Museum

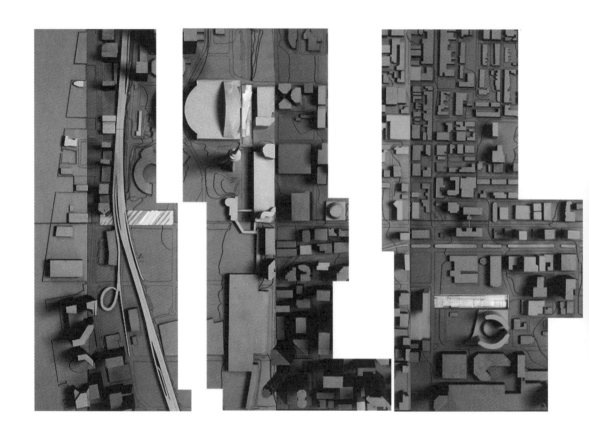

GE: J. Haliburton
City Construct

RY: S. Lee
Exposures

CH: A. Soppelsa
Square Edge

The Railway site (RY) brushes the edge of the Domed Stadium and almost reaches the land-locked base of the CN Tower. It fills the elevation gap between the train tracks and the city while linking the Peter and John Street bridges.

THIS COMBINATION: J. Haliburton's 'filtering' City Construct; S. Lee's 'threading' Exposures; A. Soppelsa's 'weaving' Square Edge; S. Ning's 'striating' City Museum City; K. Thompson's 'flooding' Culvert Link; J. Grebenc's 'scarring' OUTpost

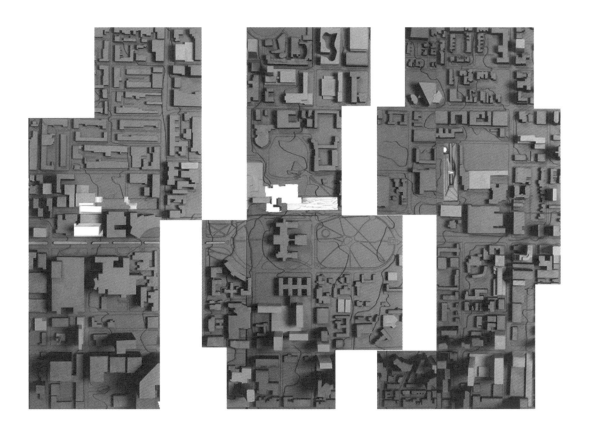

HB: S. Ning
City Museum City

QP: K. Thompson
Culvert Link

PW: J. Grebenc
OUTPost

corroding + threading + weaving + striating + colouring + scarring

One of ninety-six combinations for City Museum

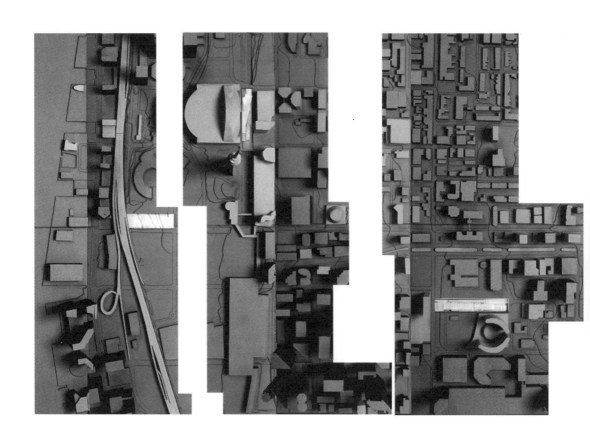

GE: E. Van Ziffle
Gardin Fronts

RY: S. Lee
Exposures

CH: A. Soppelsa
Square Edge

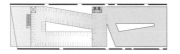

The Nathan Phillips Square site (CH) flanks the iconic Toronto City Hall built in 1965 and opposes the textured 1972 Sheridan Centre across the street. It bridges the subterranean concourse level to the street/square to the 'piano nobile' of the Sheridan Centre while reconnecting Chesnut and Queen Streets.

THIS COMBINATION: E. Van Ziffle's 'corroding' Gardin Fronts; S. Lee's 'threading' Exposures; A. Soppelsa's 'weaving' Square Edge; S. Ning's 'striating' City Museum City; L. Jeneroux's 'colouring' Tainting the Bucolic; J. Grebenc's 'scarring' OUTPost

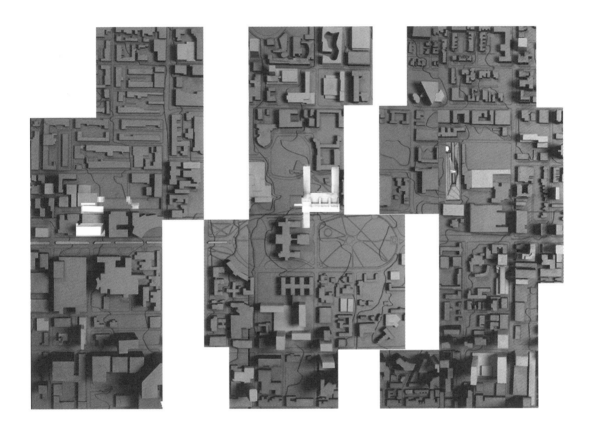

HB: S. Ning
City Museum City

QP: L. Jeneroux
Tainting the Bucolic

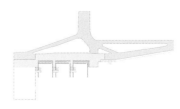

PW: J. Grebenc
OUTPost

filtering + filleting + weaving + striating + delaminating + channelling

One of ninety-six combinations for City Museum

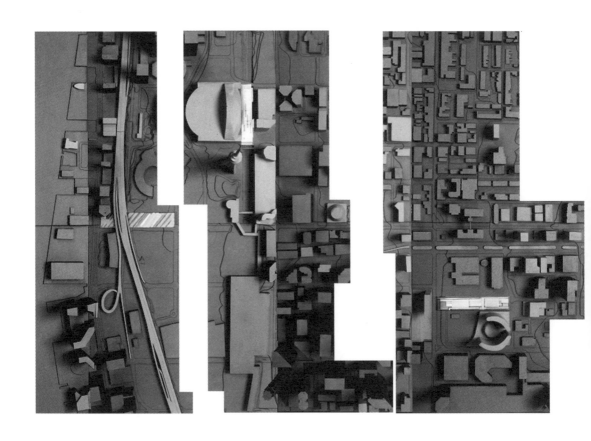

GE: J. Haliburton
City Construct

RY: T. Genshorek
Sky Beach

CH: A. Soppelsa
Square Edge

The Hydro Block site (HB) skims across the back of the elegant concrete slab of Mount Sinai Hospital and meets the end of the Hydro Block's towering broken-rib precast panels. It reconnects College Street's medical students to University Avenue's teaching hospitals.

THIS COMBINATION: Haliburton's 'filtering' City Construct; T. Genshorek's 'filleting' Sky Beach; A. Soppelsa's 'weaving' Square Edge; S. Ning's 'striating' City Museum City; V. Graham's 'delaminating' Masked; G. Chien's 'channelling' Moving Pictures

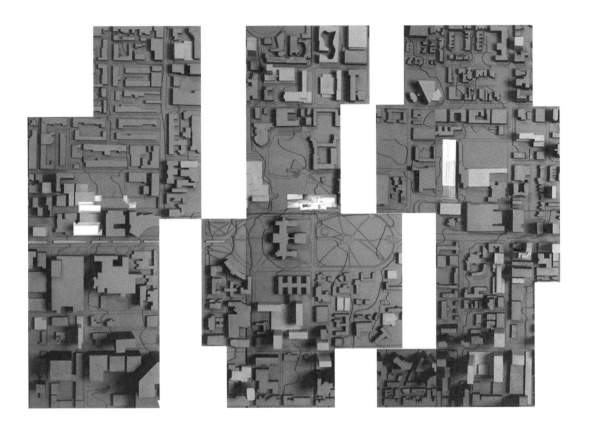

HB: S. Ning
City Museum City

QP: V. Graham
Masked

PW: G. Chien
Moving Pictures

filtering + threading + snagging + stretching + colouring + scarring

One of ninety-six combinations for City Museum

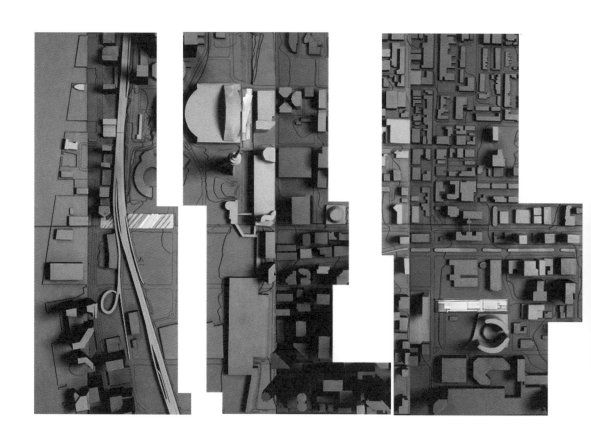

GE: J. Haliburton
City Construct

RY: S. Lee
Exposures

CH: A. Miller
Formal Glitches

The Queen's Park site (QP) is in the valley of what used to be Taddle Creek, whose upper rim is flanked by the University's 1969 Medical Sciences Building, 1962 Sidney Smith Hall, and 1974 John P. Robarts Library. It negotiates the slope between UofT's Hart House Green and the City's University Avenue.

THIS COMBINATION: J. Haliburton's 'filtering' City Construct; S. Lee's 'threading' Exposures; A. Miller's 'snagging' Formal Glitches; L. Woofter's 'stretching' Seventh Floor Ground; L. Jeneroux's 'colouring' Tainting the Bucolic; J. Grebenc's 'scarring' OUTPost

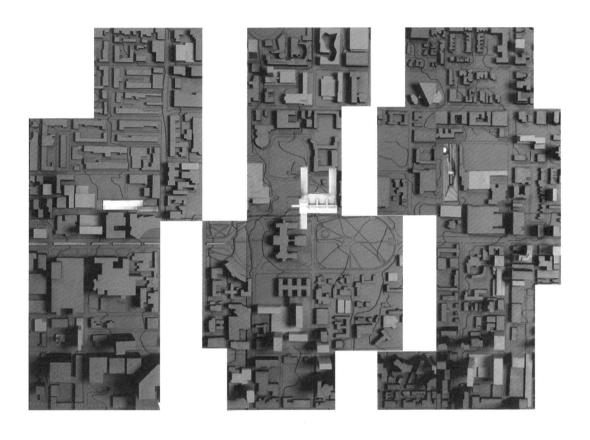

HB: L. Woofter
Seventh Floor Ground

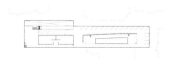

QP: L. Jeneroux
Tainting the Bucolic

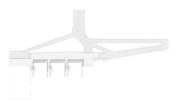

PW: J. Grebenc
OUTPost

corroding + filleting + snagging + stretching + flooding + channelling

One of ninety-six combinations for City Museum

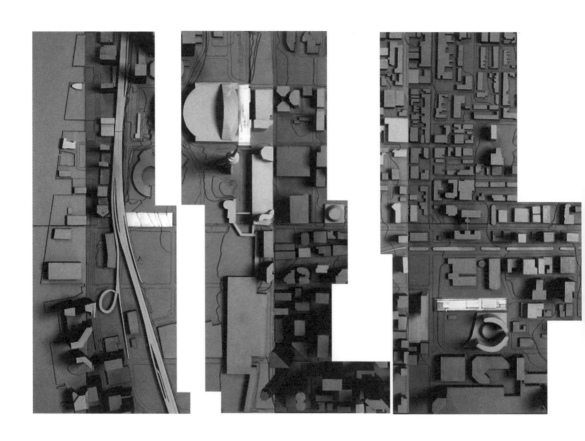

GE: E. Van Ziffle
Gardin Fronts

RY: T. Genshorek
Sky Beach

CH: A. Miller
Formal Glitches

The Philosopher's Walk site (PW) rubs shoulders with the University of Toronto's Edward Johnson Building and the newly renovated concrete bleachers of Varsity Stadium and has an axial relationship with the eccentric OISE-UT. It negotiates the space between the depressed bucolic Philosopher's Walk and Devonshire Street at city level.

THIS COMBINATION: E. Van Ziffle's 'corroding' Gardin Fronts; T. Genshorek's 'filleting' Sky Beach; A. Miller's 'snagging' Formal Glitches; L. Woofter's 'stretching' Seventh Floor Ground; K. Thompson's 'flooding' Culvert Link; G. Chien's 'channelling' Moving Pictures

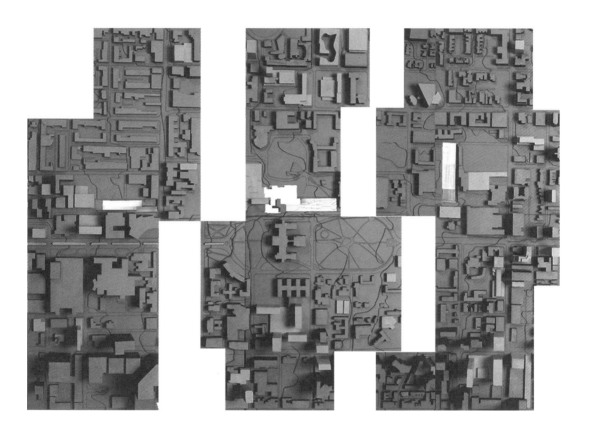

HB: L. Woofter
Seventh Floor Ground

QP: K. Thompson
Culvert Link

PW: G. Chien
Moving Pictures

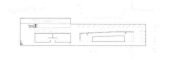

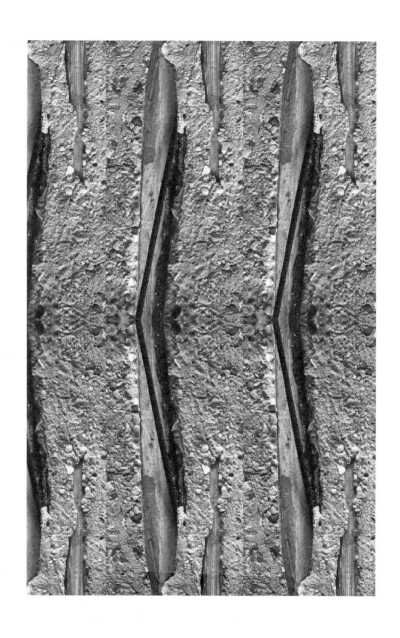

Jessie Grebenc
Abstraction of Philosopher's Walk

Concrete Insertion – Manulife Centre, Toronto, under construction as seen from Yonge and Bloor Streets; 1960s.

SECTION

-noun
'a thin slice of a tissue, mineral,
or the like, as for microscopic
examination'

'section,' definition #8. Dictionary.com, Random House

A concrete mixture is consistently composed of cement, water, aggregates, additives (in the pre-mixing stage,) and admixtures (in the mixing stage). The seemingly infinite permutations and subtle nuances of this constantly advancing recipe imply an equally inexhaustible set of possibilities for designers. Unlike wood or structural steel, concrete as a building material does not automatically imply a set of tectonic details. It is 'monolithic, omnidirectional and homogeneous in consistency' and can be adapted to meet specific and various functions and performance needs/standards through the manner of its production.[1] This must go hand-in-hand with a self-conscious approach to the formwork, which moulds the concrete and ultimately defines its tectonic language and finally the identity of its surface as it assumes the impression of its mould.

We can and always have depended on concrete to keep buildings dry, to store heat and to protect them from fire and noise. Beyond these properties that depend on its basic composition, natural density, and inherent inertia, even subtle changes to the aggregate, type of reinforcing and inclusions in the admixtures can transform or exaggerate some of its assumed properties.

Along with the perfection of engineered solutions to satisfy performance ambitions, creative, more sustainable technologies must develop to serve aesthetic experimentation – one that hypothesizes inherent shifts in meaning.

1. G.Pfeifer, A.M. Liebers, P. Brauneck, *Exposed Concrete: Technology and Design* (Basel, Boston, Berlin: Birkhauser, 2005) p.8

1966

section

Paul Rudolphe
*Government Service
Centre, Boston,
Massachusetts*

a shop-finished approach to the broken-rib panel, developed
fully in the early 1960s as an efficient rain-screen cladding
system with an inherent texture

2006   **Concrete Curtain**
Memux

supporting material of malleable, lightproof geo-textile and
individual pillow-like concrete bodies store heat, and allow
movement and protection from the sun, wind or light

Ultralite Concrete

Lightweight concrete is possible through a variety of methodologies and techniques. ACC, sometimes known as autoclaved aerated concrete, is made with all fine materials; nothing coarser than finely ground sand. What makes ACC different from lightweight aggregate concrete is that ACC contains millions of microscopic cells that are generated during the manufacturing process. In addition, ACC is unlike many other concrete products because it can be drilled, sawed, chiseled, nailed, or screwed using conventional carpentry tools.

"We believe that ultra-lightweight concrete is one of the most fundamental bulk materials of the future."

Christopher Alexander & Associates,
"A Pattern Language" Oxford Press, 1977, page 958

A scanning electron microscope image reveals the porosity of ACC concrete's structure even at the nano-level.

VERDiCT
long life concrete

Viscosity Enhancers Reducing Diffusion in Concrete Technology (VERDiCT) researchers have sought to double concrete's usable lifespan. They reasoned that rather than changing concrete's pore size, they should look to change the viscosity of the solution in the concrete at the microscale to reduce the speed at which chlorides and sulphates enter the concrete. Using small molecules (less than 100 nanometres in diameter) as additives blended in admixtures composed of lightweight sand effectively slows the creep of efflorescence and extends concrete's service life.

"Swimming through a pool of honey takes longer than making it through a pool of water. When additive molecules are large but present in a low concentration, it is easy for the chloride ions to go around them, but when you have a higher concentration of smaller molecules increasing the solution viscosity, it is more effective in impeding diffusion of the ions."

Dale Bentz Engineer
*National Institute of Standards and Technology
(February 23, 2009). "Viscosity-enhancing
Nanomaterials May Double Service Life Of Concrete."*

Image shows the slow creep of ions in a
high viscosity long-life concrete.

TX Active®
smog eating cement

The technology called TX Active®, developed by Italcementi has been proven to reduce pollutants (nitric oxides and dioxides, sulfur dioxides, carbon monoxide) by about 50%. Referred to as 'smog-eating' and 'self-cleaning' this invisible concrete coating, which is a blend of titanium dioxide that acts as a photocatalyzer, can be incorporated in cement, mortar, paints, and plaster. Essentially, in the presence of natural or artificial light, the photocatalyzer significantly speeds up the natural oxidation processes that cause the decomposition of pollutants.

"From now on in new constructions and in the restoration of large urban surfaces it will be necessary to take this new material into account. (Given) the limited amount of TX Active® cement used and its positive environmental and social impact - (it is) completely compatible with those carried out with traditional materials."

Italcementi Deputy General Manager Fabrizio Donegà
as quoted in Press Release Milan,
February 28, 2006

Virtually invisible, the TX Active coating on Richard Meier's *Dio Padre Misericordioso* defies the graying pollutants of Rome, and remains "white."

tower renewal
project:
plasticity revisited
Graeme Stewart

**Stewart 'unpacks' the cultural
status of now aged international
style apartment blocks, and
speculates on how technological
restorations can lead to new
architectures which shape new
identities.**

London

Chongching

Moscow

I: The Reigning
Concrete Tower

In his introduction to the session 'Tower and Slab' at the 8th International Conference of the European Association of Urban History, Florian Urban of the Institute of Metropolitan Studies at TU-Berlin, states that the modernist concrete slab or tower in the park type apartment building, "is perhaps the most successful typology of the modern movement". Although having faced a contentious legacy, this opinion reflects the remarkably global scope of the implementation of the ubiquitous modern tower. From Soviet mass housing, European post-war reconstruction, North American urban renewal, the utopias of Brasilia and Chandigarh, and Hong Kong's super-blocks, this modernist machine for living is truly a global type, and has largely fulfilled its mandate of providing well serviced and equitable housing for tens of millions of people.

The widespread adoption of the rationally constructed modern concrete tower in a 'park' or 'landscape' setting occurred in the context of housing shortages, central city over-crowding and tenement conditions of immediate post-war Europe. Reconstruction was not simply the process of rebuilding, but rather creating new societies, new democracies, and in the case of Britain, a new classless society in which the "mass unemployment and absolute poverty of the 1930s was impossible".[1] This strong idealism allowed for experimentation, and the acceptance of new modes of living. The modern concrete tower was the architectural and material response to these ambitions.

Offering modern amenities and conveniences, large suite sizes, as well as unobstructed access to light and air, outdoor community recreation space and 'breathing room' in the context of high-density multiple housing, the modern concrete tower was felt to be the housing model that combined the best standards possible with a responsible use of land and economic means of production.

Furthermore their regular forms and rational construction lent themselves to mass production and economies of scale; rendering the equitable provision of modern housing within the reach of fledgling welfare states, for whom the 'housing question' was a pressing concern. Endorsed by architects, planners, sociologists, economists and even health reformists[2], the modern concrete tower became a new international benchmark.

The raw aesthetic became a symbol of stability and progress following the devastation of the war; divorced from both historical fussiness and elitism on one end, and tenement slums on the other, rational façades offered the promise of modernity, new lifestyles and a new world.

Lead in many respects by the planning innovations of the 'post-Corbusiers' at the London County Council and their continental counterparts, concrete mass housing schemes became of national significance to politicians and policy makers in Paris, Berlin, Moscow, and the world over; becoming the predominant mode of urban development for the next quarter century.

The tower block's fall from grace has been as epic as its original global dissemination. A focal point of the turmoil of social clashes of the late 1970s, 80s and 90s, - and more recently the Paris riots, these aging concrete icons have entered a dubious position in the global collective conscious.

Much of the stigma assigned to these buildings in past decades is infused with notions of 'environmental determinism'; the belief that the buildings themselves have an innate and irreparable ability to negatively impact its inhabitants and surroundings. This perception was perpetuated as dogma for decades[3], and was used to justify the mass demolitions of projects such as Chicago's Cabrini Green and St. Louis' Pruitt-Igoe.

Yet recently, this near mythical view of architecture's ability to influence behaviour has been challenged, both theoretically and empirically. Commenting on socially sensitive London council houses, Trevor Allen from the Commission for Racial Equality states; "It's not the buildings themselves,

rather than the larger structural context contributing to lack of community cohesion, social capital, avenues for upward mobility, and generally low neighbourhood self esteem[4]. Following this logic, in the case of Pruitt-Igoe or Cabrini Green, it was the symbol of a social failure that was triumphantly demolished, not its root cause.

As discussed in *Concrete Toronto* regarding brutalism in general and Toronto's significant collection of concrete high-rise housing – we now suffer a cultural amnesia about this period; remaining critical yet uninformed about this architecture and leaving its very large impact on our environment without thoughtful assessment[5]. It is time to take a closer look.

As diverse as the geographies in which towers were implemented are the local responses and relationships to these structures. Encompassing, in some cases, opposing means of production, position in the housing

market, ownership, maintenance histories, and purpose, this homogeneous housing form exhibits divergent cultural meanings globally and even within urban zones.

While many of America's concrete towers continue to disappear, many of South America's have maintained the luxury status. Throughout Europe these buildings make up a considerable share of the housing market, and in many post-Soviet areas they make up the majority. While much of this stock is associated with problematic social conditions, the slab housing conditions are in fact remarkably mixed and complex. In Western Europe this housing stock is predominantly used to assist the economically disadvantaged, while in Eastern Europe and Russia it enjoys incredibly mixed tenure and is home to a large percentage of the middle class. Throughout Europe, mixed ownership, massive scale redevelopment and liberalization of land use restrictions to encourage entrepreneurship have all been strategies in evolving and rendering apartment districts as functional housing for today's context.

Perceived usefulness of these buildings is tied to the cultural relationship to them. The associated value of yesterday's icons of progress is often simply a function of the effectiveness of stewardship.

This is reiterated by Hungarian planner C.K. Polonyi, in response to criticism of a modern housing estate he helped erect in Budapest in the 1970s. 'Originally', he states 'everyone hated the five story apartments which required the destruction of two story housing at the turn of the 20th century...now we call this the historic city'[6]. He feels the negativity shown towards the modern blocks too will pass, and that their eventual legacy will be their effectiveness as quality housing, with every possibility of being as diverse and valued as the 'historic' variety.

We may in fact be experiencing the beginnings of a 'brutalist revival', or at least a revival of appreciation of the era's built form. As evident from Post-Soviet art exhibits[7], Swedish designer bed sheets, Facebook groups, German 'Plattenbau' trading cards, the now iconic status of Goldfinger's Trellick tower (including themed designer dish set), and renewed valorization of local modern protagonists the world over, brutalism is experiencing resurgence as a topic of discourse and cultural production. (This book is an example.)

This nascent renaissance of appreciation for post-war housing is not surprising in the context of the past decade's resurgence of both high-rise living and modern design. However, a critical differentiator of today's 'marketable modernism'[8], and our inherited post-war modern heritage, might be described as housing ethic. While the reductionist aesthetic of the now ubiquitous 'brick on slab' may have improved profit margins for developers and reduced costs for housing authorities, it was in keeping with the international housing ideal; meeting best practices in housing standards through

prudent and efficient means while effectively providing housing for hundreds of thousands. Although this led to a homogeneity, which ultimately resulted in the widespread rejection of the type, it was in a spirit of equality, or at least perhaps equity, that housing standards were established, and the provision of affordable multiple housing was an aspiration of societies globally.

It is hoped that as legacies of modern housing gradually become issues of collective interest, a wider critical discussion of housing generally may emerge. Moreover, this emerging process of discovery of our modern legacy may help illuminate the genuine nature of our cities; revealing the human stories and immense human potential found within. Indeed, the monotonous façades of our modern towers conceal what Doug Saunders has termed our 'arrival cities'[9] – unparalleled conglomerations of global diversity found in the outskirts of Paris and Amsterdam, East London, and the inner suburbs of Toronto – currently an issue of keen interest to Canada's National Film Board[10]. The enormous cultural potential of these evolving communities has only just begun.

The pervasive presence of the concrete tower is a remarkable legacy of 20th Century mass production. As stated by Miles Glendinning in this introduction to *Docomomo Journal 39*, "[concrete towers] serve as a reminder that there once existed an approach to city building that actively tried to reconcile the twentieth century forces of democratic collectivism and individualism, within a landscape that combined open-ended freedom with a restrained urban monumentality".[11] The negotiation of these relics with the quickly evolving 21st Century is resulting in new cultural production, architectures, and urbanisms. They, indeed, remain fundamental aspects of our evolving fabrics, and demand our thoughtful consideration.

II: Intervention / Innovation: Moving Forward

"...In Toronto...the continent's private enterprise-dominated housing system, when coupled with a structure of strong regional planning dedicated to the fostering of high-density 'hot spots' in the centre and periphery, succeeded in generating a landscape of massed towers and slabs in open space, almost rivalling the USSR in consistency and grandeur"[12].

Within the global tower diaspora of the modern tower block, Toronto, Canada is an interesting case. Between 1950 and 1980, more modernist slab apartments were built in Metropolitan Toronto than anywhere else in North America, particularly in its expanding suburbs. Promising a modern lifestyle and 'Jetsons' living, the modern tower became a symbol of progress to a young and confident nation experiencing rapid growth following the war. Aided by a strong planning regime concerned with integrating high density housing as a key component of suburban expansion, coupled with capable development companies, and an eager consumer base, nearly 2000 modern concrete towers were built in the Toronto region during the post-war boom; many were planned as satellite towns containing dense tower clusters on the urban periphery. Exhibiting a European typological and spatial approach to suburban mass housing, yet utilizing an American style free-market methodology for its implementation, Toronto exhibited a hybrid approach to post-war city building unique to North America.

Collectively the Toronto region's concrete tower stock houses over one million people[13]. However, for the past several decades, this distinguishing characteristic of modern towers and their neighbourhoods have garnered little attention in the City's collective consciousness.

This may soon change. Recent research exposing significant liabilities of this housing stock, including rapidly growing poverty and socio-economic polarization[14], and poor building performance responsible for significant greenhouse gas production[15], has brought this housing stock to the attention of urban planning and related circles. Tower Renewal, or Tower Neighbourhood Renewal, is an emerging response to these challenges, proposing significant reengagement with this modern heritage for social, environmental, and economic gain[16] – and in the process provide a venue for architectural, landscape and urban innovation.

There is a risk, of course, that ill-conceived intervention will produce less than desirable results. Generally viewed as a regional liability, too often this modern legacy is considered a problem to be fixed rather than a foundation for positive revitalization and reinvestment. Without properly understanding the found condition, it is difficult to engage with it in a meaningful way. Reframing these buildings' position in the public's imagination is key to the ultimate success of any remediation strategy.

Global Condition and International Response

Throughout Europe, the community-building and carbon-cutting potential of these aging towers has been identified and has reached varying levels of actualization. Mixed ownership, massive scale redevelopment and liberalization of land use restrictions to encourage entrepreneurship have all been strategies in evolving and rendering apartment districts as functional housing for today's context. As Europe was highly influential in Toronto's adoption of modern towers as a strategy for suburbanization, recognition of their varied response to their continued relevance seems an appropriate strategy.

In both Eastern and Western Europe, aging welfare state and Soviet-era towers have been exploited for their energy-saving potential to help achieve increasingly strict EU environmental policies. One example is in Bratislava, Slovakia. Here, the entire Petralka, a district south of the Danube River with hundreds of blocks built in the 1970s, is undergoing extensive environmental upgrades to meet new EU standards.

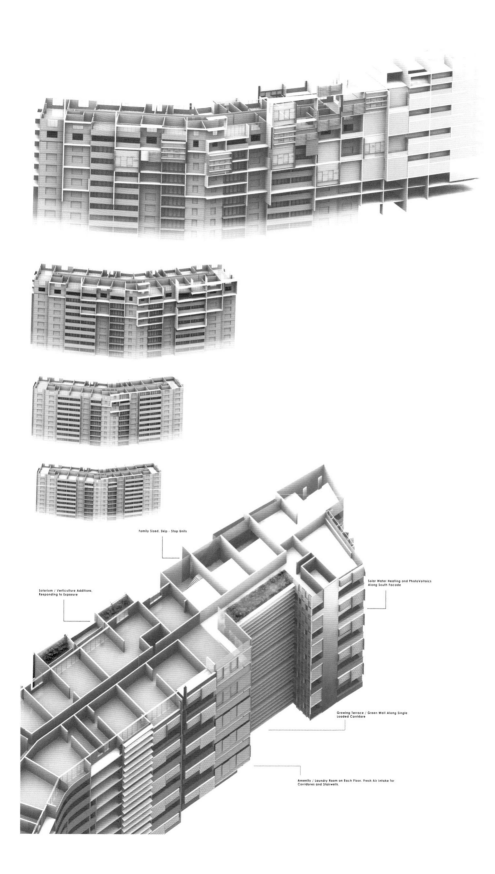

Family Sized, Skip - Stop Units

Solarium / Verticulture Additions,
Responding to Exposure

Solar Water Heating and PhotoVoltaics
Along South Facade

Growing Terrace / Green Wall Along Single
Loaded Corridore

Amenity / Laundry Room on Each Floor. Fresh Air Intake for
Corridores and Stairwells.

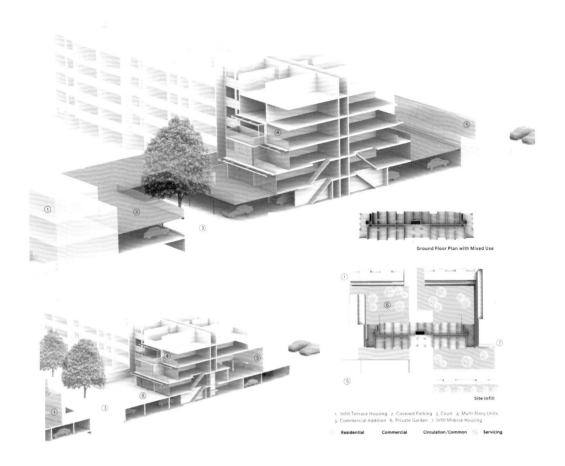

Ground Floor Plan with Mixed Use

Site Infill

1. Infill Terrace Housing 2. Covered Parking 3. Court 4. Multi-Story Units
5. Commercial Addition 6. Private Garden 7. Infill Midrise Housing

Residential   Commercial   Circulation/Common   Servicing

Paid for in equal shares by the EU Commission of the Environment, the municipality and private investors (who gain development rights on adjacent properties), the project is breathing new life into this aging district[17]. Projects of a similar scale are underway throughout the EU.

While too often these tower upgrades utilize aesthetically questionable re-clads, many are elegant, and a handful are remarkably comprehensive urban-investment projects worthy of emulation. In these examples, aging tower districts were completely reimagined through new infill development, public space and landscape upgrades. They have become popular neighbourhoods for young families; they include cultural facilities, markets and, in the case of London, even successful urban agriculture. Of particular note are the Bijlmermeer (Amsterdam, NL), Marzahn (Berlin, Germany), Swiss Cottage (London, UK) and Topli Stan (Moscow, Russia).

New Architectures

"Different forms must be sought out, not for the sake of form – but to change the content of the forms – and this will create new forms."[18]
George Candilis, 1991

When walking through a modern tower block neighbourhood, one can't help but be struck by the sheer monumentality of these structures; heroic statements from a by-gone era. The ambitious generative principles that led to the development of these modern planned communities remain relevant today. They offer a remarkable context for reengagement.

Close examination of these 'tower in the park' sites is in some senses like visiting a half completed project. It appears as a concrete frame with block walls on an expansive, though empty site, completely devoid of programme. Their inherent flexibility, both in building structure and site plan, suggest the opportunity for the reconfiguration of unit layouts, program elements, and ground plane spatial arrangements in response to evolving needs and contexts.

However they are far from a blank canvas. Superficially homogeneous, each has incredibly unique neighbourhood histories, and cultural specificity[19]. Opening these areas up for reengagement, while maintaining the integrity of social and cultural outcomes, will require the careful balancing of ecological, heritage, and community objectives. Engaging this significant modern legacy in a manner responsive to built and cultural heritage will provide an opportunity for significant new cultural production as well as new modes of architectural, urban, and landscape practice.

Building performance upgrades will dramatically reduce greenhouse gas production, and also foster aesthetic innovation. Options include building over-cladding, as explored in detail in the Tower Renewal Guidelines[20] as well as complementary enhancements including but not limited to district energy production, solar walls, and 'verticulture' installations. These sites can become a testing ground for leading approaches to green refurbishment practice.

This form of reengagement provides an opportunity to build on modern principles and aesthetics; providing a foundation for new layers of formal responses to today's functional demands (from solar shading to waste chutes). As new modes of production, materials and functional requirements evolve, the aggregate of this reengagement will lead to new architectures.

Engaging surrounding open space to address evolving neighbourhood programs provides an opportunity for innovation in site planning and urban organization at both the immediate site and neighbourhood scales. Rather than rejecting the original site intentionality outright, this reengagement can lean heavily on a rich tradition of modern open space design from Roehampton's picturesque landscapes, to the human scaled urbanism of Bakema's Lijnbaan in the Rotterdam city centre[21] which, containing small shops, cafes and cinemas, is, according to Mumford, 'exemplary in almost every way'[22]. Similar principles were also used in Sweden's seminal Vällingby, which created a public commercial centre of great intimacy within a satellite housing project consisting largely of high blocks.

Without resorting to historicism or anti-modern rhetoric, these successful examples of modern planning point to integrating an expanded modern canon into the interventions of our aging modern districts. Similarly, in engaging the landscape, 'place making' and productive landscape can bring a renewed relevancy to the 'tower in the park.'

What may ultimately become the most achievable and significant interventions, could be the 'informal architectures' created through the simple liberalization of land use controls, enabling what Giancarlo de Carlo might consider 'liberating operations of disorder.' This is indeed the case in tower sites across Eastern Europe and Russia, where the proliferation of individual actors has given former dead zones a 'carnivalesque' atmosphere and enhanced community and commerce, resulting in remarkable new forms of ready-made urbanism in the context of aging concrete towers.

At the regional scale, numerous global examples demonstrate that carefully retrofitted, post-war apartment districts can emerge as hubs for community activity, energy and food production, waste management, transport, growth, and service delivery; providing cost effective services and resource networks for the community, the City and region as a whole. Applied comprehensively, thoughtful reengagement can have a significant impact on consumption, travel patterns, resource management, greenhouse gas production, and most importantly, foster vibrant, equitable and diverse communities throughout the region.

Modern Heritage and the Next Toronto

Buildings go through cycles, at least one's relationship to them does. This is evident in the shift of the Victorian urban landscape from 'utterly reviled' to a 'much loved vernacular heritage[23]' that took place during the 1970s, and is perhaps in the early stages for the post-war concrete building stock in question.

Toronto's famous rejection of modernism has for better or worse defined much of its collective urban psyche – or cultural myth – for the past quarter century. As we once again are faced with the need to embark on large scale regional planning exercises to ensure continued high-quality of life and economic prosperity, the intrinsic value of our modern legacy becomes apparent, born of similar conditions 40 years ago.

Perhaps our acceptance, revaluation, and reappropriation of this significant modern heritage, will define our notion of our post-war cities, and their relevance to an increasingly shifting world, in the decades to come.

1. Frederick Shaw. *The Homes and Homeless of Post-War Britain.* London: Parthenon Press, 1985. VIII
2. Miles Glendinning. "Ennobling the Ordinary, Postwar Mass Housing and the Challenge of Change" *Docomomo 39, Postwar Mass Housing.* (Docomomo International, Paris: 2008) 6.
3. Interview: Dennis Sharp, Dennis Sharp Architects, *Docomomo England,* London, September 2006
4. Interview: Dennis Sharp, Dennis Sharp Architects, *Docomomo England,* London, September 2006.
5. Michael McClelland, Graeme Stewart. "Foreword". *Concrete Toronto: A Guidebook to Concrete Architecture from the Fifties to the Seventies.* (Toronto: Coach House Books, 2007). 12.
6. Cor Wagenaar. *Happy: Cities and Public Happiness in Post-War Europe.* (NAi, 2005) 504.
7. Such as the 'Hotel Neustadt Installation' www.hotel-neustadt.de
8. Miles Glendinning. "Ennobling the Ordinary, Postwar Mass Housing and the Challenge of Change" *Docomomo 39, Postwar Mass Housing.* (Docomomo International, Paris: 2008) 10.
9. Doug Saunders. *Arrival City: Toronto.* Knopf Canada, 2010
10. A glimpse was recently documented in the National Film Board's *Thousandth Tower* documentary, showcasing six residents in a dynamic tower community in suburban Toronto.
11. Miles Glendinning. "Ennobling the Ordinary, Postwar Mass Housing and the Challenge of Change" *Docomomo 39, Postwar Mass Housing.* (Docomomo International, Paris: 2008) 10.
12. Miles Glendinning. "Ennobling the Ordinary, Postwar Mass Housing and the Challenge of Change" *Docomomo 39, Postwar Mass Housing.* (Docomomo International, Paris: 2008) 7.

13. Graeme Stewart, Jason Thorne, *Tower Neighbourhood Renewal in the Greater Golden Horseshoe.* Toronto: Government of Ontario, 2010.
14. For more information on Toronto's growing economic disparity, see: David Hulchanski, *The Three Cities Within Toronto: Income Polarization among Toronto Neighbourhoods.* 1970-2000 Toronto: Centre for Urban and Community Studies, University of Toronto, 2007.
15. For more information on Toronto's high-rise energy performance, see Ted and Ivan Saleff, "Differential Durability, Building Life Cycle and Sustainability". 10th Conference on Building Science and Technology, Ottawa, Canada. May 2005.
16. For a full account of the advantages and opportunities of Toronto's modern concrete towers, please refer to the *Mayor's Tower Renewal Opportunities Book*, 2008, and the University of Toronto's *Tower Renewal Guidelines*, 2009.
17. Interview: Dr. Slachta, Head City Architect, Bratislava, September 2006.
18. "The difference between good and bad" *Team 10: In Search of a Utopia of the Present.* Ed: Max Risselada and Dirk van den Heuvel. Rotterdam: NAi.
19. See David Bezmozgis. *Natasha and Other Stories.* (Toronto: Farrar, Straus and Giroux: 2004).
20. *Tower Renewal Guidelines.* Ed: Ted Kesik and Ivan Saleff, Daniels Faculty of Architecture at the University of Toronto, CMHC.
21. Sarah Williams Goldhagen and Réjean Legault (eds.), *Anxious Modernisms: Experimentation in Post War Architecture and Culture.* (Montreal: Canadian Centre for Architecture, 2000).
22. Lewis Mumford, *The City in History.* (New York: Harcourt, 1961) 459.
23. Miles Glendinning. "Ennobling the Ordinary, Postwar Mass Housing and the Challenge of Change" *Docomomo 39, Postwar Mass Housing.* (Docomomo International, Paris: 2008) 9.

Weston, Ontario

section

Eric Van Ziffle
Abstraction of Gardiner Expressway

notes on section

Canadian developments of concrete technologies, such as the continuous pour technique of the CN Tower's slip form, made it possible to have an entire temporary concrete mixing plant mounted on site to avoid transportation issues and obtain a steady stream at high volume. With summer temperatures like those of Mexico City and winter temperatures that match those of Helsinki, Toronto's unusual climatic challenges require a unique focus on customizing the performance of this provocative material. Each proposal for these chosen sites adopted then altered current material technologies to critically assert a new voice among the whispers of their concrete context.

Sky Beach at Rail Yards site

Tangie Genshorek

Section 2: Railway Yards

At the depressed railway yards, below the mammoth Rogers Centre's domed stadium, Tangie Genshorek's Sky Beach utilizes a geothermal service core which skewers a series of concrete trays. Its labyrinthine thermal coil stores then slowly releases heat where various leisure activities defy seasonal limitations in the open air. Accessible by car, bicycle and foot, the outdoor pools/ice rinks utilize a strategic profile of conductive concrete where its concrete mix contains micro steel fibres and steel shavings for stable electrical conductivity – enough heat is generated to selectively prevent ice formation on the concrete pavement.

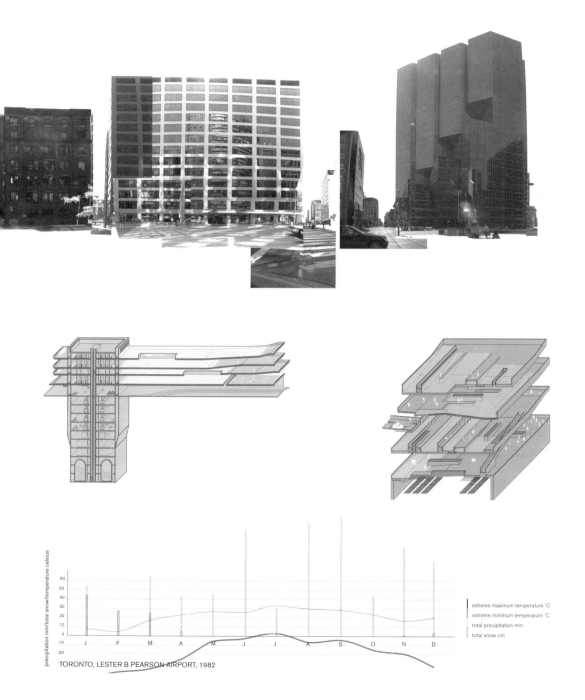

precipitation mm/total snow/temperature celsius

													extreme maximum temperature ˚C
													extreme minimum temperature ˚C
													total precipitation mm
													total snow cm

60
50
40
30
20
10
0
-10
-20

J F M A M J J A S O N D

TORONTO, LESTER B PEARSON AIRPORT, 1982

Gardin Fronts at the Gardiner site

Eric Van Ziffle

Section 1: Gardiner Expressway

Foreign Office Architects' Phylogenesis strategy is reinterpreted by Eric Van Ziffle's Gardin Fronts to inhabit the super-thin concrete housing for a car rental/auto park/bus station structure at the edge of the raised expressway. It ultimately creates an artificial ecology, a series of 'lungs', where cars' CO_2 is consumed by vegetation, which in turn excrete O_2 into the air. Organized as a coupled ramp system, centre hollows and staggered floor plates give relief to an otherwise lightless, deep and compressed concrete parking garage that celebrates the tension between parks creating a giant filter between the lakefront and the city.

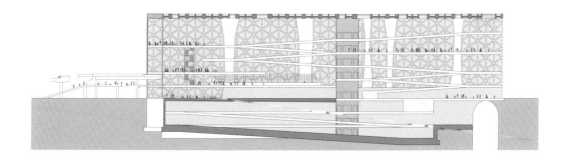

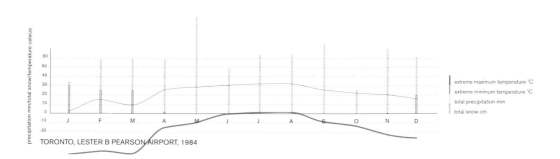

precipitation mm/total snow/temperature celsius

60
50
40
30
20
10
-10
-20

J F M A M J J A S O N D

extreme maximum temperature °C
extreme minimum temperature °C
total precipitation mm
total snow cm

TORONTO, LESTER B PEARSON AIRPORT, 1984

Culvert Link at the Queen's Park site

Kenzie Thompson

Section 5: Queen's Park

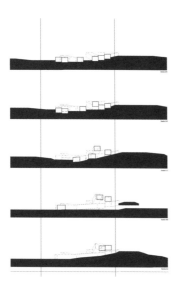

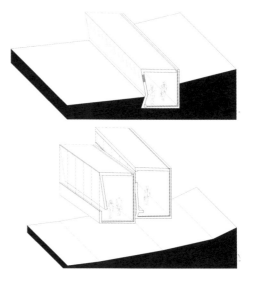

'Impervious concrete' where water-based sealers are added to the concrete mixture in order to impregnate the concrete throughout its thickness, defines Culvert Link by Kenzie Thompson where concrete culverts are virtually uprooted in the absent flood of Hart House Circle at the University of Toronto. The culvert-like tentacles are instruments of an elaborate grey-water management

and recovery system, which employs a 'smog-eating' photocatalytic concrete coating. This nanometre thick clear coating, developed by Italcementi, which has been proven to reduce air pollution in urban areas by 50% with only 15% coverage, is strategically distributed to allow only select moments of weathering – making the invisible visible.

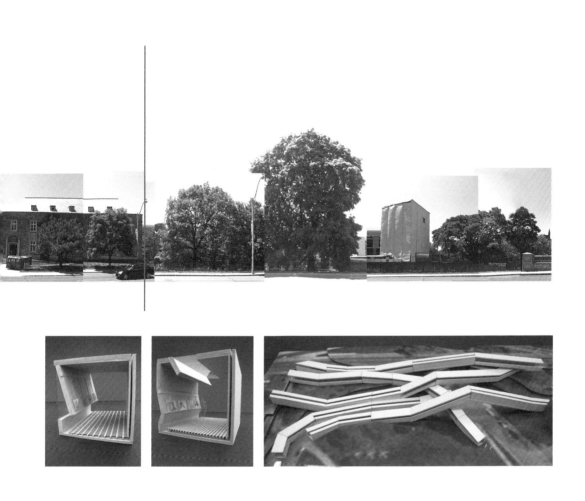

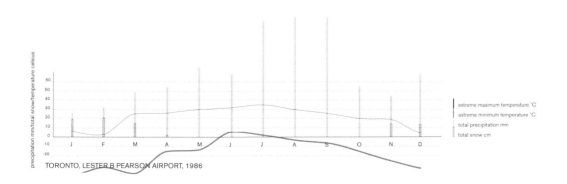

precipitation mm/total snow/temperature celsius

60
50
40
30
20
10
0
-10
-20

J F M A M J J A S O N D

extreme maximum temperature ˚C
extreme minimum temperature ˚C
total precipitation mm
total snow cm

TORONTO, LESTER B PEARSON AIRPORT, 1986

Square Edge
at the City Hall site

Alessia Soppelsa

Section 3: City Hall

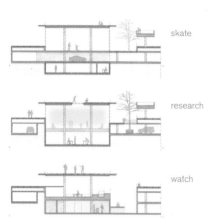

skate

research

watch

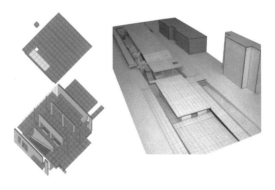

The relentless concrete plaza is no longer blistering and bleak. Square Edge by Alessia Soppelsa literally adopts these strategies of short-chain repellants and surfactants to experiment with readings of a crafted concrete, which exaggerates requisite qualities of repetition and texture. The relentless drainage tray system gets delaminated at times, to support new concrete 'squares' that assume identical proportions and the identities of their 1960s counterparts, however the manipulation of their molecular make-up unleashes a destabilized, new reading. A series of concrete tile 'imposters' with translucent and rear projection concrete are combined with a sprinkling of nanosensors to render the weightless extension of the civic square as a shallow textured galleria.

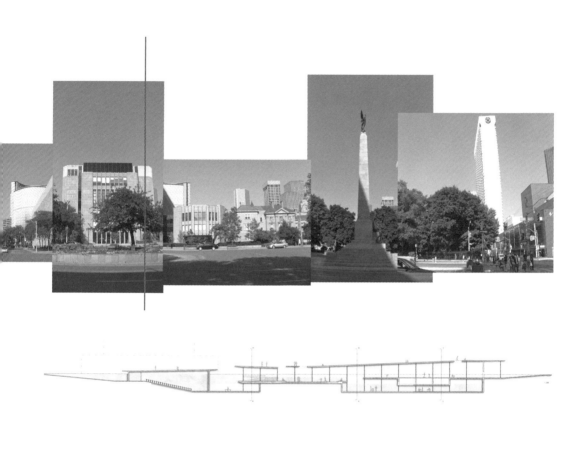

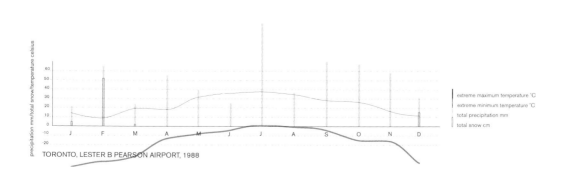

TORONTO, LESTER B PEARSON AIRPORT, 1988

extreme maximum temperature °C
extreme minimum temperature °C
total precipitation mm
total snow cm

precipitation mm/total snow/temperature celsius

60
50
40
30
20
10
0
-10
-20

J F M A M J J A S O N D

Masked at the Queen's Park site

Vanessa Graham

Section 5: Queen's Park

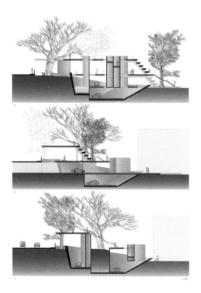

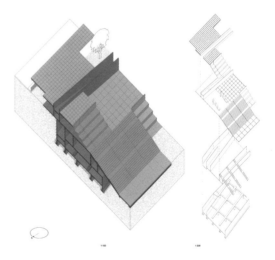

Masked by Vanessa Graham veils the steep edge of Queen's Park Boulevard and Hart House Common to manage the 'muck' and create a dialogue between the lower campus and the upper city. The result is a re-conceptualized concrete plaza, which resists a bleak, cold reading in the greyness of winter. Rather, a two-way hollow deck which utilizes plastic balls ('Bubbledeck') to reduce the use of concrete that has no carrying effect, is utilized to achieve clear span cantilevers that defy its expected weight. In addition, built-in photovoltaic lenses collect daylight to release an evening glow along the plaza.

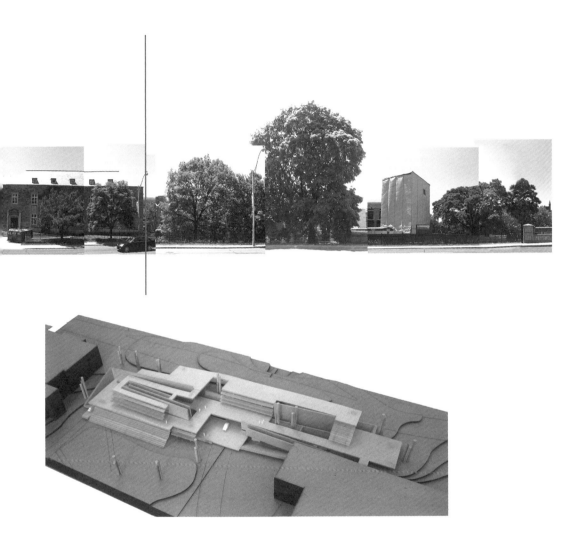

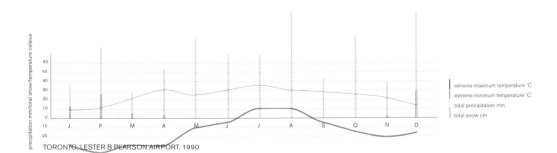

TORONTO, LESTER B PEARSON AIRPORT, 1990

precipitation mm/total snow/temperature celsius

60
50
40
30
20
10
0
-10
-20

J F M A M J J A S O N D

extreme maximum temperature °C
extreme minimum temperature °C
total precipitation mm
total snow cm

City Museum City at Hydro Block site

Shi Ning

Section 4: Hospital Alley

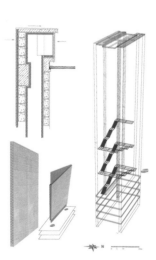

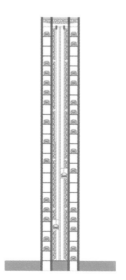

At the Hospital Alley section of concrete laden University Avenue, Shi Ning's City Museum City proposes strategies for thermal storage, utilized for comfort concepts that save energy and render an outdoor concrete space habitable even during inhospitable weather. Since an adequate temperature rise or drop must occur between daytime and nighttime, additional daytime heat is borrowed from cars and bodies for the necessary magnification of sunlight. Via labyrinth-like concrete coils, heat is stored for slow release. In this case, this entombed chamber system is integrated in a parking structure and incorporated in a heavy-handed structural system. In others, the system is spread like a landscape element that sets a new earthen ground plane – warm in winter and cool in summer.

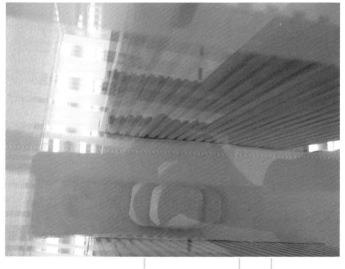

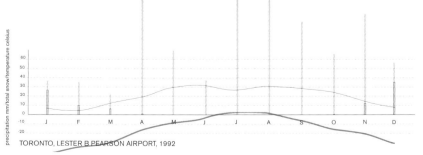

precipitation mm/total snow/temperature celsius

60
50
40
30
20
10
0
-10
-20

J F M A M J J A S O N D

extreme maximum temperature ˚C
extreme minimum temperature ˚C
total precipitation mm
total snow cm

TORONTO, LESTER B PEARSON AIRPORT, 1992

OUTpost at Philosopher's Walk site

Jessie Grebenc

Section 6: Philosopher's Walk

A ductile ribbon of insulated concrete that unravels from a subterranean anchor to a cantilevered, precarious belvedere negotiates the change in grade from the low-level, damp ravine of Philosopher's Walk to the upper street-level of the city. Jessica Grebenc's OUTpost utilizes concrete laden with reinforcing microfibres for an outstanding strength-to-weight ratio. This allows the concrete cantilever above ground to be remarkably thin, while subterranean retaining walls are reinforced to resist hydrostatic pressure from the creek bed and are embedded with drainage conduits to manage the natural swell during periods of thaw.

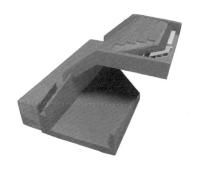

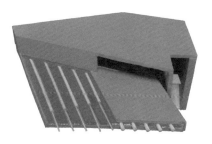

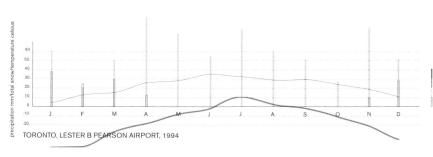

TORONTO, LESTER B PEARSON AIRPORT, 1994

precipitation mm/total snow/temperature celsius

60
50
40
30
20
10
0
-10
-20

J F M A M J J A S O N D

extreme maximum temperature ˚C
extreme minimum temperature ˚C
total precipitation mm
total snow cm

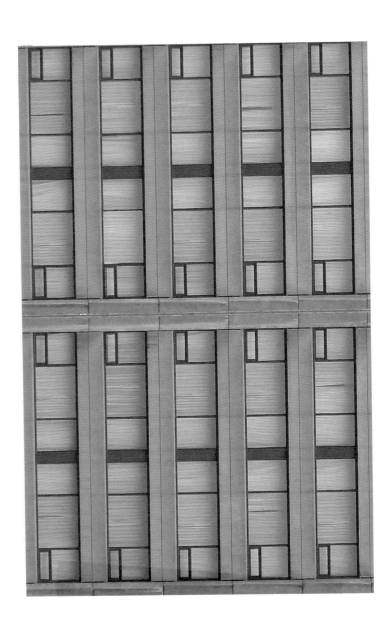

Anne Miller
Abstraction of Nathan Phillips Square

SPECULATION

-noun
'assumption of unusual risk in hopes of obtaining commensurate gain.'

'operation,' definition Legal a. Dictionary.com, Random House

Can the more self-conscious tectonic innovations of concrete, such as strategic interventions of infrastructure, building and surface afford new presence to existing concrete architectures by providing the lens through which we perceive and experience them? This question begs further questions about an inherent cultural specificity afforded by any building material. What Kenneth Frampton refers to as 'critical regionalism', a building strategy whose aim is to reflect and serve the limited constituencies in which they are grounded, seems to pertain directly to the search at the level of nano-technologies for new versions of concrete. Directives to adjust the performance of concrete seem to come from specifics in climate, geography, social values, economy, and traditions – factors that define cultural specificity.

We can therefore speculate on current material questions in architecture that do not limit themselves to technology and building performance, rather they extend to psychological, cultural and aesthetic techniques. For example: If material is a form of thinking in architecture, how does one define material research that is outside conventional questions of technology and experiments and concerned instead with questions of authority, perception and aesthetic culture?

Further, given the now mainstream nano-technologies that transform the performance of materials at the molecular level without fundamentally changing the material aesthetic, can we anticipate a shift in its cultural status? Ultimately, concrete might look the same but it is no longer burdened by its unsustainable, gravity-ridden heaviness.

1 Kenneth Frampton, *Modern Architecture: A Critical History* (London: Thames & Hudson, 1997) p.314

1968

Kallmann, McKinnell, Knowles
Boston City Hall

civic monumentality is achieved only by the self-referential aspects of Brutalism

1966   **van den Broek
& Bakema
Aula of Delft**

formwork and poured-in-place concrete render an
'honest' finish

2005

EMBT
Scottish Parliament

complex robotic technology solved the challenge
of creating bespoke precast panels, cloaking the
Canongate Wall with new civic monumentality

Impervious Concrete

3001, by Nanovations, is a water-based solution that is added to the concrete mix and used to prevent the creep of water through micro cracks and capillaries. Previously, surface sealers and penetrating impregnations were used after concrete was poured and set, with limited results and several reapplications required. By impregnating the concrete throughout its thickness, this new sealer becomes a permanent part of the concrete and is unaffected by surface abrasion.

"3001 is completely water-based and VOC free. This is the long awaited technology to avoid millions of gallons of polluting solvents currently used in penetrating sealers. The product has been tested for salt resistance, efflorescence, water absorption and frost/thawing behaviour."

Harry Stulajter, Director of Nanovations
Industrial Manufacturing News August 31, 2007

Surface detail of impervious concrete.

LiTraCon®
light transmitting concrete

The optical effects of LiTraCon®, a translucent concrete, are the result of the inclusion of thousands of optical glass fibres into the fine concrete mix that form a matrix and run parallel to each other between the two main surfaces of every block, becoming a structural component as a kind of modest aggregate. Comprising only 4% of the total volume these glass strands transmit an ethereal light and thus have both ornamental and structural properties.

"In theory, a wall structure built out of the light-transmitting concrete can be a couple of metres thick as the fibres work without any loss in light up to 20m. Load-bearing structures can also be built from the blocks as glass fibres do not have a negative effect on the well-known high compressive strength of concrete."

LiTraCon inventor, architect Áron Losonczi
LiTraCon website

Precast LiTraCon® block detail.

Self-healing Concrete

Bacterial Mineral Precipitation suggests that concrete can self-heal cracks by using calcite-precipitating bacteria. Using extremely pH resistant bacteria, researchers have been able to create concrete environments that have self healing properties. Self healing concrete reduces the need for additional costly steel reinforcement or frequent and unsightly repairs.

"We found, to our happy surprise, that when we load it again after it heals, it behaves just like new, with practically the same stiffness and strength. Self-healing of crack damage recovers any stiffness lost when the material was damaged and returns it to its pristine state. The material can be damaged and still remain safe to load."

Victor Li,
E. Benjamin Wylie Collegiate Professor of Civil Engineering, University of Michigan

SEM image shows bacterially produced robust, 20 - 100 μm-sized, calcite-like precipitates required for crack repair.

questions
1-4

Experts in their field, Will Bruder, George Elvin and Mark West respond to complex questions about the shifting status of material concrete in our collective consciousness in the contemporary city.

question n°1:
material research

If material is a form of thinking in architecture, what for you constitutes material research that is outside conventional questions of technology and experiments but rather lies with questions of authority, perception and aesthetic culture?

Will Bruder

For me, concrete has always been a material of the place. It becomes how we define our culture and our place and our technology and our time. In my own search for architecture as I build in various parts across America and in other places in the world, I always try to get into the context of what each place represents as a materiality. It's interesting that this is evidenced from the time of the Romans, to the time of Louis Kahn, a master in concrete. Kahn's amazing concrete work raised the idea of concrete to a whole new profound quality and to a sort of Yeoman's standard, that rivaled any precious material, inspired by some of that work in Toronto from the 1960s and 1970s. This became, I think, concrete 'at the time' – it was all about a velocity and an appropriateness to what appeared to be a technology of our time. This view was inspired by Le Corbusier and Louis Kahn. It was just a material of resource that also fit the economy of our perception of a new architecture, of some permanence, and was then raised to the level of high art.

George Elvin

One thing that I try to do with the organization that I run, Green Technologies, is look at the research and frame it in the way that I think this question suggests. We ask: what are some of the cultural implications of researching new materials and how do we bring that into the community of practice and into the aesthetic of architecture? For example, I gave the closing talk a couple of years ago at a symposium called The Nanotechnologies and I was the lone designer at that symposium in Bilbao.

All the other presentations were by scientific researchers on specific experiments on the material properties of concrete. It was wonderful because they were bringing up all these new ideas about concrete and new ways to use concrete, looking at it from a purely technical point of view. You know, tweaking the number of nanotubes they are adding to their concrete mix and what does that do to the tensile strength – those kind of questions. Understandably, not because they are scientists and they have their own interests and expectations, I come with Green Technologies Forum into the environment of scientific research, in the realm of its own interests and expectations, as a kind of bridge between research and practice.

Mark West

It's a funny question because I guess I'm not sure what conventional questions of technology are. At least in a major portion of our research, the material is actually our instructor and our imagination, the material does a good deal of the imagining for us. Steven Vogel is a biologist and he wrote a book called *Life in Moving Fluids* which is about his area of research. In that book, right at the very beginning of it he describes his research method like shooting a shotgun against the wall and then drawing bull's-eyes around all the holes. When I read this I thought that's exactly it! That's how I work. I guess that is my answer to the question of a material's inherent authority, whatever that's worth. This is the method you might call basic research. If you take a material – in this case concrete, and its mould – in this case fabric or another flexible membrane, by simply playing with the materials like closing your eyes and shooting the shotgun against the wall and waiting for something to happen, a series of form eruptions can occur. This is what we have been doing for the past 18 years or so.

Will Bruder

When Habitat came along in Montreal, people got really inspired by the fluidity of this material full and ripe with form possibilities, with making possibilities and with the speed of industrialized formwork at a time when our culture held different values about energy. There was probably not a lot of thinking about the implications of this brute mass material with regard to what would follow. I think this gets to the core of the question. Concrete became the material for infrastructure, the material for transportation systems, the material for the foundations of a whole complex, and if material is a form of thinking in architecture, it ultimately became a material of resource that also fit the economy of our perception of a new architecture, of some permanence. In Canada this was a totally optimistic time with the work of Arthur Erickson in the Western provinces and Vancouver, and John Andrews' Scarborough College for the University of Toronto was artful but it was a concrete manifestation – no pun intended – of the visionary unbuilt work of Santa Elia. We must consider that John Andrews, from his period at Harvard, where he witnessed the construction of Le Corbusier's Carpenter Centre right before his young student eyes, carried with him all optimism of concrete technology. I think that as I look at this question now, I can't help thinking that as architects we know more now about the material science of making and of thermal implications and working in the context of a green world. In the end, it's the seduction of a material that talks about a new way to think about concrete. There's this translucent concrete now that's been envisioned so that for every jury we sit on at every university everybody wants to do the translucent concrete building right? You don't even have to question – "why would concrete ever want to be translucent?" You know, just because we can, do we do it? What does it become is the bigger question.

George Elvin

I take the various new exciting research in areas like nanotechnology and biotechnologies, that are so strongly influencing materials already, and think about how they might be impacting the whole aesthetic of a building. This is really exciting for me. To see that now as we build up the Forum and draw in partners from practice and from research where the practitioners are really excited too about picking up some of these innovations that are coming out and applying them in their practice. Similarly, any scientist takes great satisfaction in seeing their experimental work actually applied in the world. Of course when you are talking about the construction of concrete – when we use more concrete than any other material by weight in the world – and so if these people can come up with something that expands the way that we use concrete then they would get a lot of satisfaction from that. People at the Nanotechnologies Conference were representatives from US Gypsum, BASF – huge companies that are also extremely interested in applying some of these ideas. They were very enthusiastic, particularly from a 'green' point of view. A lot of the work going on in nanotechnologies and biotechnologies right now is geared towards making material greener, and in concrete a lot of the experimental work going on right now has to do with not adding new material but if you, for example, grind Portland cement to a nanoscale – a nanometer which is a billionth of a metre – to a much finer powder that goes a lot further as an adhesive in the mix. They are finding that this process can actually cut the amount of Portland cement in the concrete mix in half and still have a strong concrete. And, as you probably know, cutting the amount of Portland in half will have huge environmental implications because the production of Portland cement accounts for such a huge concrete energy footprint.

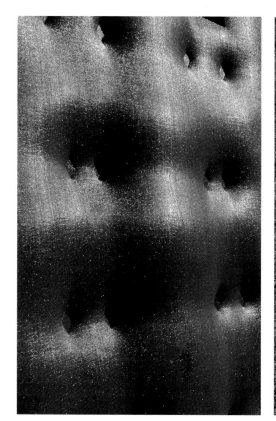

Mark West's fabric forms also leave an indelible imprint on cast concrete surfaces where even the grain of the fabric is visible to the naked eye.

Traditional cast-in-place wood board-formed concrete bears testimony to the history of its making.

The Medical Sciences Building at the University of Toronto has a sculptural façade of thick precast concrete. Meticulously cast panels designed by the artist Robert Downing in six variations create the illusion of a randomized composition.

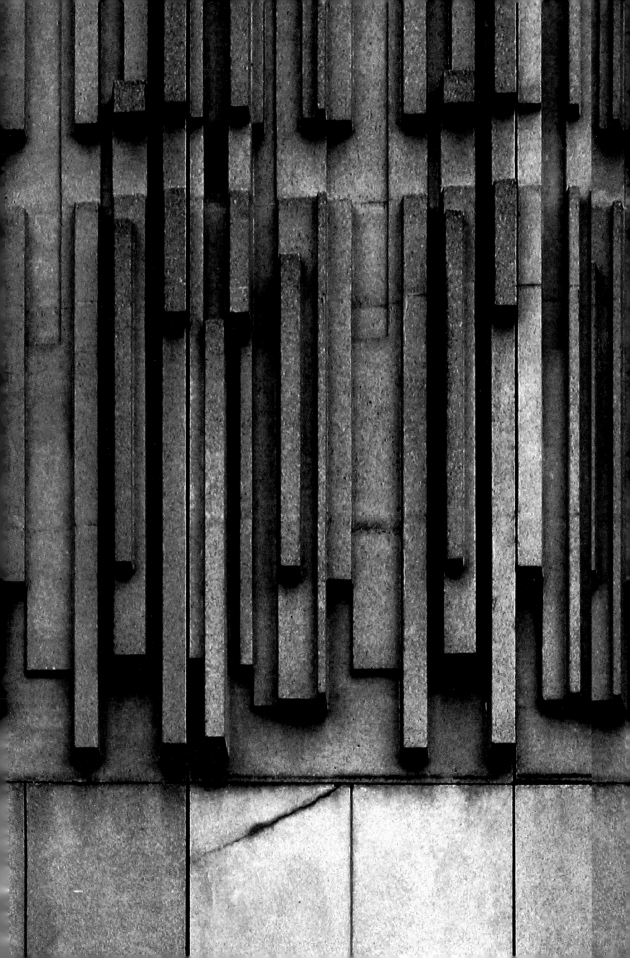

Artist Max Lamb creates his sculptural stools by turning ultra light foamed concrete (ACC) using a traditional lathe and woodworking tools. Crafted by hand, each piece bears a unique geometry.

question n°2:
inherent psychology

As it is so often cited, likely for its utilitarian (vein or grain-less) renditions, can a material such as concrete be categorically 'cold?' And a material such as wood be categorically 'warm?' These definitions seem to depend on an inherent psychology rather than an inherent performance of the material. How can we experiment with the complexity of these tectonic expressions of the material?

Will Bruder

I think that this idea of cold or warm has an awful lot to do with both sensual perception and realities of character of the moulded forms we make. Any material gets its life through an inventor and architect and artist, a sort of underlaying of ideas as to why the material was chosen, why it exists, and how you interpret it through its making, whether in the celebration of the technology or the hand that crafted those forms or made those surfaces, and what they have to do with scale and proportion. We have so many formless, scaleless, ill-proportioned buildings in the landscape. It's not for a lack of craft necessarily, it's all in the ability of the designer to interpret and celebrate craft to the worth of their idea. The case I can make right now is for a building, like many of the buildings of its period, a building of the sixties and seventies that I was involved in analyzing. It was a library in Salt Lake City that was built from 1963 to 1965, and it was ordered, carefully looked at one level, it was competent and simple – it was case book for every building that we saw from California to Toronto to Montreal to New York City to Atlanta.

George Elvin

That, I think, is going to be one of the biggest changes in the architecture of the 21st Century. From everything that I have seen and everything that is already occurring in areas like nanotechnology and especially biotechnology, the nature of the material is not so much inherent

anymore. Essentially, if we see a thing growing or existing in the ground as a natural resource and take it and work with it, yet work with it through technologies such as these, we are redesigning materials. That is very much happening right now in areas like bioplastics where organic materials are grown actually with the intent of making things like packaging or building materials out of them. So, we are starting to design materials as born out of an idea or, as National Labs put it, "we're not designing with materials anymore, we're designing materials from the atom up", and so whether it's concrete or wood or glass or plastic (whether it be inorganic or organic), we are increasingly designing them with new performance characteristics. We haven't gotten to the luxury yet, let's say, of designing for aesthetic characteristics because most nanomaterials and biomaterials tend to be more expensive than their more traditional counterparts.

Mark West

I don't think the inherent psychology of a material is so divorced from the performance of the material. I have a phenomenological approach to thinking about that and the performance of a material, like for example, if there is a piece of marble in a room and there is a piece of wood in a room and you touch the wood and it's not cold, and you touch the marble and it is cold, even though they are both the same temperature right? So that's the performance of the material that would lead you to feel that wood was warmer that stone, concrete, or metal. That's the performance of the material that makes the thing warm or not in terms of your psychological attitude or perceptual impact or the phenomena of it. So these things are not separate, and the fact that you walk on a wood floor that creaks, or you walk on a concrete floor that doesn't creak, is part of its performance. You could use the word performance either in a technical sense – as its thermal mass or thermal conductivity as in the first instance, or you could use it in the theatrical sense in that these characters inhabit or make up our built world and are performing all the time.

Will Bruder

No one in the community loved this building. When you talked about it as a 'piece of architecture', it captured no one's fondness or memory or anything, and it was so curious because you could see that there was a certain competency and carry in the architecture and yet about 800 miles away from this site in Salt Lake City is San Diego and you have a building that was crafted from 1963 to 1965, the Salk institute by Louis Kahn. It is iconic, one of the great architectural achievements of all of mankind. Certifiably. So, what is the difference between the two buildings? What makes something like the Salk institute transcend the obvious shortcomings in the Salt Lake City Library? Kahn's building was about an idea – it was about these surfaces in the sun and the way that the every nuance in the form and the marking of forms and the joints, of the movement and the virtual proportions and scale of every wall plane were orchestrated with the light – from the way that it grew from the ground to the way it kissed the sky. I mean these are things that are inspired, and you know there are few things like that, that happen. On the other end of the spectrum, we can look at La Tourette or Chandigarh by Le Corbusier. Even in their 'shoddiness', there is a magic that prevails because of the largeness of the ideas and aspirations of these buildings. So, it's not just that concrete has become a poor man's stone, that it either needs to be treated with such perfection of intention or with just such rawness and directness,

but the majority of the buildings are just normative (without ideas), concrete just chosen to fulfill the function of structure and enclosure. This idea of perfection of craft versus perfection of rawness or poetry in these buildings by Le Corbusier is critical to answering this question. The concrete block is a smaller scale manifestation of this material 'in your own backyard'. An interesting and artful attempt is made in the work of Massey Dubois as well as Ron Thom to translate the brute force of the material into a more romantic evolution of surface and texture. Learning from some of the best traditions of Scandinavia and other colder, greyer climes, Erickson, Dubois, and Thom made remarkable attempts to reach something that was romantic and warm and understood as almost man-made stone. Their buildings really weathered quite interestingly. There is one part of our culture – with an almost Eastern reverence for materials – that has a strong attitude about what age and patina and weathering is all about. And another part of our culture that is more Eastern European, Germanic, if you will, isn't really willing to accept the idea of the weathered barn – it's the barn that's freshly painted once a year. Concrete is like that weathered wood building that some of us have a love affair with, and others see as falling apart and shoddy. Generally, we don't accept weathering, whether it's our body or our character, as it is a distinguishing characteristic of time. We want to call up the plastic surgeon, we want to do these other things to ourselves to deny that truth – and concrete is a material that almost demands a truthfulness. It's something cultural. I know in my country, America, we strongly influence the anti-idea. To accept this material because it is so honest and straightforward, and yet, we have not become an honest culture. We have become a culture of temporal fashion and style that doesn't really ground itself in these other things.

George Elvin

The research is really targeting improved performance characteristics. I mentioned before some of the greener materials. Bioplastic is a good example because that is made from organic materials like farm residues rather than from petroleum. By environmentally improving the strength of the material so it goes farther, as well as improving the life cycle costs because they are more durable, more and more of the builder's and architect's palette is open to design. We're going to see some of the patternizations or labels suggested by this question, like 'concrete is cold', 'wood is warm', because there is going to be so much more that wood or concrete or brand new materials that we have created from the atom up are capable of. The diamond is no longer the world's hardest material – because there is a race among nano-technology labs to create harder materials and they have; and keep outdoing each other. There is constantly a new 'world's hardest material' and so I would see that through the 21st century we will certainly see materials that will make concrete look warm by comparison or wood cold by comparison. Again, by designing materials from the atom up it will be quite amazing what we can come up with.

Mark West

If you look at a material completely objectively, and take a look at what is happening to a material at any time, it is prodigiously active. It's constantly active. Its surface is exchanging molecules and atoms at a prodigious rate. It's always engaged, some more than others, so wood might have sugars that are breaking down that become food for some animal, or the metal is oxidizing although these things are happening at a much slower rate than we might be able to perceive except over time. The nature of their activity is in the aggregate which is completely perceptible to us. We know these materials. We know wood as wood and that it is different from concrete. So the performance of concrete, its physical nature – its hardness, its temperature, coldness and so forth – is all bound together in that it corresponds to its psychological sense so there is no getting away from it. Raw concrete, if you dump it out on the ground with no container, no modulation, no anything – it's just this ugly clump of gravel stuck together and it's not a beautiful colour, it's rough and can hurt you if you fall on it, it gets old and it falls apart and you can't even reuse it hardly – only if you crush it up and use it as lower quality aggregate in more concrete. It's not like stone where you could cut it into smaller stones and use it again, it's just hard to work with and the mould making process is high risk and it's much more enjoyable to work with wood; for me speaking personally I like to work with wood. I don't like to work with concrete. But concrete is transformable in really miraculous ways. Now, getting to the general perception that concrete is a cold brutal material, because when I was in Architecture school we were taught that the beauty of concrete was its masculine brutality, massiveness, strength. There was an aesthetic cloud drawn around it that had to do with these kinds of qualities. That was its beauty. Well that's true if you're casting it in big rectangular chunks against rough wood, but if you put it in a fabric for example – have you ever seen fabric cast concrete in the flesh? It is amazing – it is so delicate – you can see the stitches – in fact in the days when we would sew them together with a zigzag stitch you could see the stitches of the joints. If you get a microscope you can see the twist of the fibres in the thread that you stitched it with – it is incredibly sensitive and delicate to detail. But that's only if you are treating it well. If you treat it in a delicate, yielding way, and if the fabric is a permeable fabric when you place the concrete, all the air bubbles pass through this permeable membrane and then all the excess mix water starts to pass through this permeable membrane and the membrane turns into a filter, and it starts to collect cement paste at the surface of the mould. Cement paste is one of the finest things that human beings can make in terms of its dimension – the dimension of the actual particles of cement paste are among the very smallest of things we can make. So the microscopic resolution is immaculate, if you're able to treat it in a yielding, filtering way. It just happened by chance. It wasn't my idea. We just started making things and out come these incredibly beautiful surfaces – and that's just the surface itself and the form of the thing, in these soft curves like an inflated, quilted, puffy shape. You look at it and immediately associate it with fabric, like quilted or stuffed fabric or drapery and so forth. You feel it to be soft visually and then there is this weird surreal moment when you touch it and it's hard and all your circuits get crossed and you don't know what this thing is anymore. People are more used to it now because it's been published and things have been built out of it, and so forth, but if someone's looking at it who has never seen the thing before, or expected it, there is a moment – and in the early days this would happen all the time – where people would see one of these things and as they walked towards it their hands would go up in front of them and they would touch it to confirm what the heck this might be and they would say 'Well, what is this?' And you say, 'Well, it's concrete poured into fabric,' and the question would usually then be: 'Is the fabric still on it?' And you say 'No, that's concrete,' and then you would get this blank stare; 'Like, really, that's concrete?' It's so utterly transformed from the usual concrete that they're used to – concrete cast in a rigid rectangular mould. The only reason concrete is rectangular and flat and has that texture is because of the mould material. So cast concrete as an architectural material is never alone, it's always the concrete and its mould that is the architectural material. The architectural material is 90% its mould and 10% concrete (or something like that). It's the mould that determines the architectural, let's say psychological, and let's say the perception of concrete as a material. On top of that is the material's physical character. There is not a material on earth you can't transform through craft. You can paint wood, or you leave it to age naturally and turn grey, or you oil it, or stain it or something. You can transform wood. You can transform anything but I suppose that, at least for the time being and for the foreseeable short term future, the transformative power of a fabric-cast concrete seems to be greater because we are so used to its previous technical incarnation. Rigid wood moulds for example, are still so ubiquitous. Because every piece of concrete is like that, we think that that is what concrete is like. We think that is the shape of concrete, but concrete has no shape, it doesn't have an opinion – it's the mould. So when the mould gets taken away to the landfill, the actual cause of the 'nature of concrete architecture' disappears and we are left with this illusion that is the concrete that is giving us this impression.

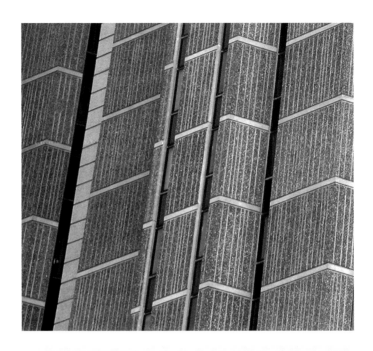

New thin-skinned Ductal panels are so flexible that new curvatures are possible and ornament, like the dimples on this project's surface, provides textural relief as if it were a kind of contemporary aggregated surface.

Robarts Library's raked concrete surface was made possible through the use of rough aggregates and rhythmical striated precast panels to render a highly articulated surface.

The University of Toronto's Athletic Centre bears the signature geometries of its fabrication – joints, anchor points, and orthogonal relationships.

question n°3:
cultural status

Given the now mainstream nanotechnologies that transform the performance of materials at the molecular level (such as smog-eating concrete coatings as well as new ductile or lightweight concrete) without fundamentally changing the material aesthetic, can we anticipate a shift in its cultural status? Ultimately, concrete might look the same but is no longer burdened by its unsustainable, gravity-ridden heaviness.

Will Bruder

Well, if we look right now at the sort of forms that are born from the application of computer software such as Form Z, like the cantilevered forms of Zaha Hadid and the sculpted 'white' masses of Greg Lynn, we find formal expression without any material quality. It could be made out of any material we come up with. The form exceeds the idea of any celebration of the materiality or its making. Is it ironic in these cases that they employ concrete because it can meet their formal needs? It's very ironic it meets their needs for certain functions – it's there. Another thing that is very interesting is that concrete again, case in point, the very brutal buildings of Paul Rudolph who is really not interested in the material at all, we see his preoccupation with the spaces formed by its sculptural qualities. Material became a choice and everyone looks at Paul Rudolph's textured block and the brutal textured concrete; whereas what he was really interested in was sculpting planes of light and shadow and form, and it seems secondary that they were made of concrete.

George Elvin

I think there will be. And you have already suggested reasons why. Concrete is a terrific material for what it can accomplish and that is one reason it has become the world's most commonplace material. I think as we move forward with new technologies, concrete will become much more versatile. I think it will become more

dynamic in that, for example, there are experiments now in concrete where carbon nanotubes, which are extremely conductive, are inserted into concrete so that you can actually use the concrete as a conductor and you can alter its appearance. It can illuminate, radiate heat, or act as an insulator bringing a lot of new performance capabilities to concrete. And, I think one thing that we will start to see in general with materials becoming more dynamic, is more intelligence and interaction. I use the term 'smart' environment. As you get more and more materials that, through the integration of nanotechtonic sensors, are much more capable of responding to their environment, to their users, and to each other, we will know more dynamic environments.

Mark West

I try to learn about new concrete technologies as well as old antique uses of lime and Portland cement and I have an interest in these things. It is not, however, something I am actually studying in my work. I'm picking stuff up from the people who work in the concrete factory and I'll ask questions, but I don't keep a file. I am not studying it, I'm not reading any books. Although it is not my area of interest, it is an associated knowledge that is helpful to me. However, if we can use less concrete not by making it stronger but by shaping it differently or more efficiently, it is worthwhile. I do feel that there is no real urgency to develop new materials as far as we are still discovering the old ones, right? So anyone who thinks that a new material is somehow going to redeem us for building, they have the wrong idea. If you look back through the history of architecture, you see that we have made the most beautiful things out of the most primitive of materials – primitive in light of our technical capacity.

Will Bruder

This became, however, another big jumping off point for the architecture of a whole generation. It's interesting how influential buildings can be. I think, right now, the 'Catch 22' of the unfulfilled dream of concrete becomes its ability to express itself in a culture with high labour costs and lagging craftsmanship impeded by this whole idea that these concrete buildings are driven by code and structural implications and the burden to virtually achieve the kind of scale of the contemporary built environment. And so I think that the 'Catch 22' is the material you don't see, yet, it's every architect's dream to do the beautiful concrete building. And I'm having a love affair with a cast concrete structure right now that goes all the way from a garage into the headquarters environment of this corporate headquarters. And it's thinking about this expression but you know it's been a major challenge to get anybody to understand or feel the passion for it. So, I think even though we are looking to some of these new technologies, for their performance, concrete is still about celebrating its base, inherent qualities. It goes back to the Romans who used concrete as a structural material, yet carried with it all the subtle nuances and variations of other technologies. I don't yet see any of these new nanotechnologies being a sweeping technology that is going to transform the way we think about concrete as a culture or as a design profession. Concrete's great thing will always be just the idea of its mass and the quality of this 'cast stone' that when treated in masterful hands, with ideas and invention, offers so much.

George Elvin

Already we are seeing things like implants in people in terms of interactions between people and buildings; there is a surveillance company in Ohio that has implanted several of its employees with radio transmitters so that they can monitor access to a particularly secure area where they store high security surveillance tapes and there are other examples of that as well. So we are certainly starting to see the signs of a much more dynamic and intelligent palette of materials that I think will add up to the smart environment of the future. I think the big question is environmental. Concrete will escape its historic perception as the heavy massive bulk that hold things up as it becomes imbued with the ability to do so many other things. Because of the environmental unfriendliness of Portland cement production, concrete is going to have increasing competition from biomaterials – though this is some ways off – but certainly at some point in the 21st century we are going to have materials made from renewable resources that can compete with concrete and concrete will compete back by becoming more environmental friendly, it will absolutely become more versatile and expand in ways as you say that counter its first stereotype or tradition as concrete as a cold heavy material that has got to improve its environmental performance in order to take that role on.

Mark West

I mean that's the architecture we all want to see when we go travelling, even if it's only a bunch of rocks piled on top of each other – you don't need a new material to make really beautiful or even fabulously efficient structures or architecture. In our intoxication with the new – it's a distraction, and the relearning of every generation has to relearn the nature of materials so that we can proceed with some intelligence and subtlety and love. If we're not paying attention to relearning it and then going on to the next new thing and the next new thing after that (which is of course a cultural addition) this older knowledge begins to decay and we are left with a series of distractions. I do speak with people in the concrete industry quite a bit and I was at a local conference in Winnipeg and they were talking about recent problems in some concrete constructions in Winnipeg

The viscous properties of the ultra-fine grained Flowstone makes layered and multi-dimensional relief possible as evidenced in these cast panels whose alien surface lies somewhere between natural sandstone and synthetic plastic.

Traditional precise concrete modules are inverted and stacked to create the heroic and organic Helix sculpture by Ted Bieler in the forecourt of the Medical Sciences Building.

and no one knew what the problems were exactly and this one guy piped up and said 'You know, we don't really know what the effect of all these chemicals that we put in the concrete is.' And I said 'You don't? ' 'Well no, not really. I mean we know what it does in terms of its performance in placing the concrete and curing and the strength that we get after 28 days but we don't know how durable it is in the long run and the effect of multiple chemicals in the admixtures etc. It's like a new chemistry set. And we don't really know.' I hadn't really thought about that myself. He's probably right, we don't actually know. In my research, in anyone's really sustainable research, OK I'll say anyone's because there are really two paths you can follow. You can work towards higher efficiencies, so higher mechanical efficiencies, higher material efficiencies and so forth, as a way of reducing material and energy consumption. And that's the way that is valorized now, there is a high value placed on higher efficiencies. But there is another way that is a more sustainable practice, and that is to use less of the same stuff. To meet higher efficiencies if you use less. It is technically easier, and therefore more accessible to more people in the world. But it is culturally impossible – impossible for current culture, it's like asking an alcoholic to just drink less – and to them it's a horrifying idea just as it is to most of us in a capitalist society. In that sense culturally, or in that sense individually, it is difficult to just consume less. But, that's the approach that I am taking.

We don't need new materials which tend to be more capital intensive in terms of production and there also seems to be a rule that the higher the technology the less robust, so you lose robustness when you become more and more refined. Higher and higher performance means lower and lower robustness. What we need now in a time of energy contraction and so forth is higher levels of robustness and to do that we have to look backwards. So to figure out how to consume less we have to look backwards. We could just look back one generation, or two generations, and get lots of information from people who lived perfectly fulfilled lives simply consuming less. If you look back more than two generations and you really go back pre-mechanical and pre-electrical and all of that, there are all of these solutions that are not standard stock of sustainable architecture – like: passive cooling, passive heating and so forth. So, I'm a little more curious these days about older ways of making concrete. Hydraulic lime, I've been told, can make a concrete that is actually stronger than Portland cement concrete – maybe you would have to wait two years for it to hydrate – which is not on our construction timeline you know – it's just too slow for us, but it has all of these advantages. There is way less embodied energy in lime than there is in Portland cement and you can reconstitute it and you could also take a lime mortar off of bricks and reuse the bricks if you wanted. It is more plastic in terms of how it functions so there are tremendous advantages to using old-fashioned lime mortars over Portland cement mortars but that knowledge is basically lost. You can't find anyone in North America in any engineering faculty researching hydraulic lime. It's too old, too antique. It's archival, but those are the technologies that really interest me in terms of their sustainable potential.

Translucent concrete mixing optical
fibres and Portland cement transcends
concrete's opaqueness allowing light to
pass unimpeded.

Cast-in-place concrete fins create a
rhythmic play of light and shadow in the
colonnade of the Larkin Building on the
University of Toronto campus.

question n°4:
virtue in unique qualities

If we can say there still exists a general perception that 'concrete still looks best, from the outside, in Mediterranean climates'; and, our -30°C to +30°C Toronto, where there are only 85 sunny or partly sunny days a year, has an unparalleled richness of Canadian shining moments in concrete – ones which do not fit the decidedly beautiful sculptural/smooth moulds of celebrated concrete buildings around the world – can we find virtue in unique qualities of (lack of) smoothness, in greyness and in ugliness?

Will Bruder

There is a big difference between concrete as structure and concrete as skin. We seem to be fascinated now with glass for example as really the building skin of our new century. All these new ways to manipulate glass with frits, with colour, with insulation, with environmental quality, and to a certain extent structure. Young and fertile minds think you can have the structural glass wall that does it all. The same thoughts captured the mind of one of the great concrete architects of contemporary times, John Lautner. Lautner thoroughly loved the material of concrete in California and was always interested in pushing the 'envelope'. For each generation concrete has been always in the background holding things up and steel is always fighting it, but steel doesn't have the same fireproofing qualities. There is therefore a directness and honesty of concrete which was one of its virtues when we did Phoenix Central Library for example. It became a Tinkertoy of precast components, yet in one stroke the structure becomes the fireproofing, becomes the architectural finish.

George Elvin

I think so – we have talked in a lot of ways about how concrete through new technologies can take on a new role that it hasn't traditionally had, but I think it could also make concrete more extreme in the Toronto tradition.

You have things like Raymond Moriyama's Canadian War Museum which plays up the rough jaggedness and roughness of concrete, and speaks to the issues of war through that; and if there were circumstances where you would want to push that further – as Moriyama might have wanted to in that same setting – I think these new technologies will make that even more possible. In general, just broadening the palette and amplifying the performance of traditional materials – concrete, glass, steel, wood – and allowing them to express themselves even more because all the way back to Frank Lloyd Wright, to Vitruvius, you name it, there is this constant battle or challenge between the architect and the available materials in terms of what we can do versus what is in the architect's mind.

Mark West

So much as to heighten the presence of this existing building stock that seems to have slipped into our urban subconscious with surgical concrete interventions? I don't think we can say this anymore – that concrete still looks best from the outside, in Mediterranean climates. In terms of heightening the presence of the existing concrete stock, in its brutal state, I'd have to say we should look to the artist Hunter Voster. Hunter Voster is a painter in Vienna, Austria, who has done these strange buildings with trees growing out of them. Weird stuff, however, he has done a series of façade remediations in Austria and elsewhere as a kind of painter-doctor. Surgical concrete interventions would have 'run deeper' so to speak – a kind of architectural doctor.

Will Bruder

When you carefully consider every piece of the 'Tinkertoy' of that precast assembly it became a language, the tectonic articulation. It was the means as well as the end. But when you look at the exteriors of buildings I think that's where we've always witnessed this other validity of expressing the new technology of the new times. I mean, look at Louis Sullivan's use of terracotta and the cast ornament façade of buildings like the Wainwright and Guarantee buildings. It is interesting because I stumbled upon this white terracotta building by Louis Sullivan a couple of years ago after having left the Rivington Hotel which is a sort of celebration of developer translucent glass – an invention of our time right? And in looking at the two buildings I suddenly realized that they were 100 years different in their birth – they were celebrating, at a different time, with a different technology, but with the same reason. The terracotta was a way that people could finally afford what they had gotten used to, stone, but could no longer afford in real stone carved surfaces – carved by all the Italian immigrants in America. It's like the great Romanesque buildings of people like AJ Richardson, reinterpreted using new technology by Louis Sullivan in the 1890s making terracotta skins and the new technology in 2010, 100 years later, where architects like Sejima, to Will Bruder, to Rem Koolhaas – you name it – are all playing around with this idea of glass and the magic variables of what glass is. And so it's interesting that we all find the material of our time and yet in the background concrete is always at the core. This headquarters I am building for Dial Henkel in Scottsdale is a totally – I mean thousands of yards of structural concrete – and yet, what are we wrapping it with? Façades, where they are expressed somewhat in concrete on the base like a great stone mass and as it reaches the sky as a crystalline cloud it is the same heavy concrete frame expressed on the inside, but wrapped as

a crystalline cloud of glass with a scrimmed fritted glass system. It is expressive, I think, in its duality.

George Elvin

Through nano-technology and biotechnology we expand the palette. It opens up a whole breadth that is not limited to just making concrete more light and fluffy, so to speak, but to counter its tradition using materials across the board, and expanding in really all directions, which is what is so remarkable. We have talked about certain examples today of what is happening in material technology through nano-technology and biotechnology and we have focused on concrete. But, across the board we will be seeing this, I think, remarkable expansion of what materials will be in the 21st century.

speculation

Today, surface texture can be applied without the use of complex moulds. Graphic concrete allows designers to make engraved surfaces through the use of a thin film that resists the curing process, allowing even the most delicate patterns to be revealed.

Alessia Soppelsa
Abstraction of Sheraton Centre

notes on speculation

Ultimately, the resulting proposals develop innovative tectonic strategies, at various scales, to positively inform the current cultural, aesthetic and sustainable status of this age-old material. Through buildable solutions, concrete is ultimately reconsidered as lush and poetic – it is afforded a new reading that is not merely utilitarian or 'cold' within the challenging boundaries of comfort set by the Canadian climate.

Culvert Link
on Queen's Park site

Kenzie Thompson

Culvert Link by Kenzie Thompson re-conceptualizes the infrastructural concrete culvert which is virtually uprooted in the absent flood of Hart House Circle. The culvert-like tentacles are instruments of an elaborate grey-water management and recovery system, which employs a 'smog-eating' photocatalytic concrete coating. This millimetre thick clear coating, developed by Italcementi, which has been proven to reduce air pollution in urban areas by 50% with only 15% coverage, is strategically distributed to allow only select moments of weathering – making the invisible visible. Each 'culvert' cracks, splits and fuses to negotiate new pedestrian and vehicular links between the upper city and the lower university campus – each framed by dense collections of forgotten objects recovered by the Toronto Transit Commission.

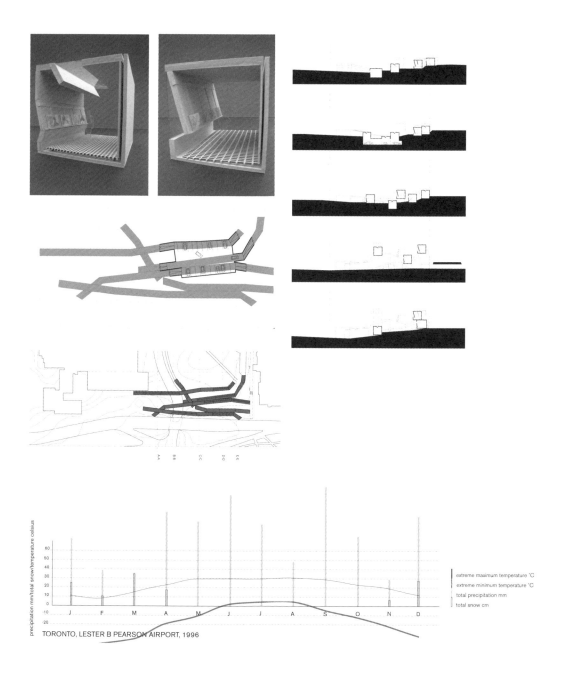

TORONTO, LESTER B PEARSON AIRPORT, 1996

extreme maximum temperature °C
extreme minimum temperature °C
total precipitation mm
total snow cm

Square Edge
on City Hall site

Alessia Soppelsa

Square Edge by Alessia Soppelsa raises, literally, the relentless grid of concrete tiles that define Nathan Philips Square in order to recover its western edge. The drainage tray system gets delaminated at moments, to support new concrete 'squares' that assume identical proportions and identities of their 1960s counterparts, however the manipulation of their molecular make-up unleashes a destabilized, new reading. In turn, the underground world selectively is allowed to surface within a palimpsest of historic urban elements. A series of concrete tile 'imposters' with translucent and rear projection concrete are combined with a sprinkling of nanosensors to render the weightless extension of the civic square a shallow galleria embedded with the history of zoning legislation in the City of Toronto.

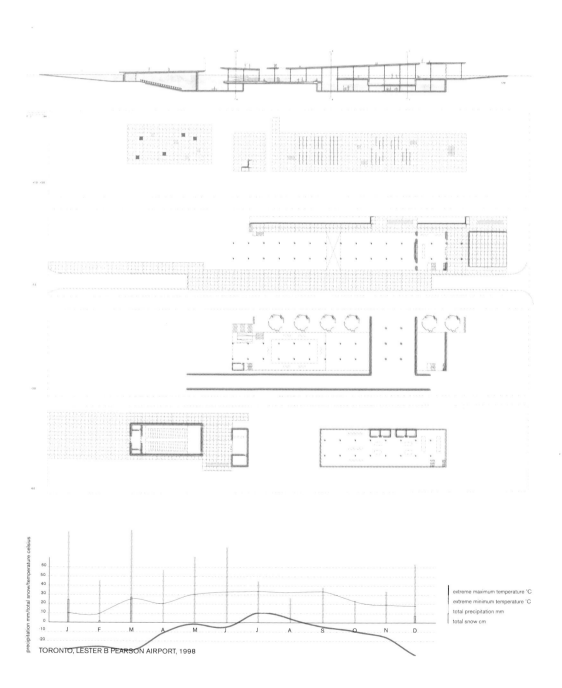

extreme maximum temperature °C
extreme minimum temperature °C
total precipitation mm
total snow cm

TORONTO, LESTER B PEARSON AIRPORT, 1998

City Museum City on Hydro Block site

Shi Ning

City Museum City by Shi Ning capitalizes on the tight spaces of the service corridors of Hospital Alley. Five concrete towers, that at first glance sport the corduroy ribbed precast panels of the nearby Hydro Block Building, opportunistically ground themselves at junctures of circulation to harness the pedestrian and vehicular currents of this busy passageway between the hospitals, the university, and the city. Labyrinth thermal storage systems, like those developed by Atelier Ten, where double coil walls of concrete are used to store heat harvested from cars and some sun, are designed with a concept of comfort in mind. To moderate heat in summer and moderate cool in winter, labyrinth-like concrete coils store heat for slow release in a series of parking/gallery towers that punctuate the background of University Avenue.

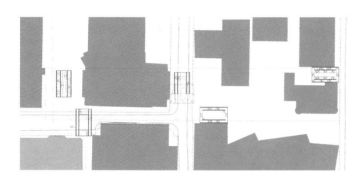

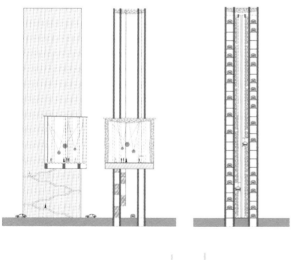

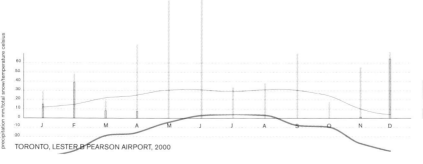

extreme maximum temperature ˚C
extreme minimum temperature ˚C
total precipitation mm
total snow cm

TORONTO, LESTER B PEARSON AIRPORT, 2000

OUTpost on
Philosopher's Walk site

Jessie Grebenc

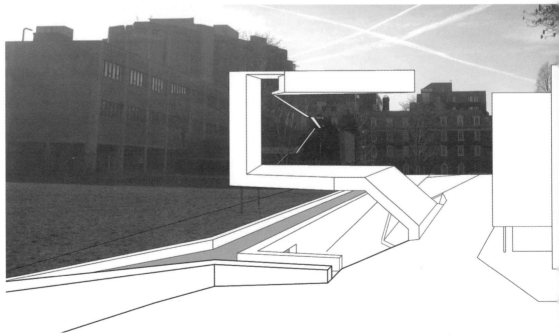

OUTpost by Jessie Grebenc deploys a ductile ribbon of insulated concrete that unravels from a subterranean anchor to a cantilevered, precarious belvedere. At the western entrance of Philosopher's Walk, a bucolic old creek-bed that strings together a series of cultural institutions where the university campus edges the city, Grebnec's partially submerged car park offers a new urban frame for near and distant views. Like a line of runaway bleachers from the adjacent Varsity Arena, the structure participates in the +twelve-metre 'canopy' of the city. Concrete is laden with reinforcing microfibres for an outstanding strength-to-weight ratio. This allows the concrete cantilever above ground to be remarkably thin while subterranean retaining walls resist hydrostatic pressure from the creek bed and are embedded with drainage conduits to manage the natural swell during periods of thaw.

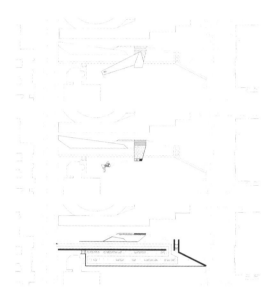
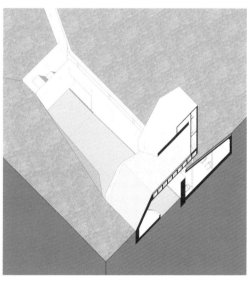

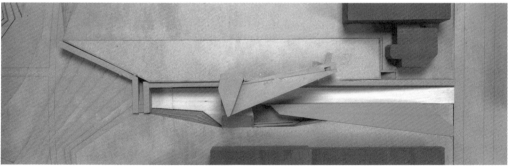

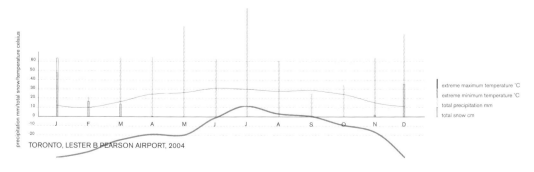

TORONTO, LESTER B PEARSON AIRPORT, 2004

extreme maximum temperature °C
extreme minimum temperature °C
total precipitation mm
total snow cm

precipitation mm/total snow/temperature celsius

Sky Beach
on Rail Yards site

Tangie Genshorek

Sky Beach by Tangie Genshorek stacks a series of concrete trays that span the urban gap created by the depressed railway lines and raised edge of the mammoth-domed sports stadium, the Rogers Centre. A geothermal service core skewers the concrete trays with a labyrinthine, thermal coil that stores then slowly releases heat where various leisure activities defy seasonal limitations in the open air. Accessible by car, bicycle and foot, the outdoor pool/ice rinks utilize a strategic profile of conductive concrete where its concrete mix contains micro steel fibres and steel shavings for a stable electrical conductivity – enough heat is generated to selectively prevent ice formation on the concrete pavement.

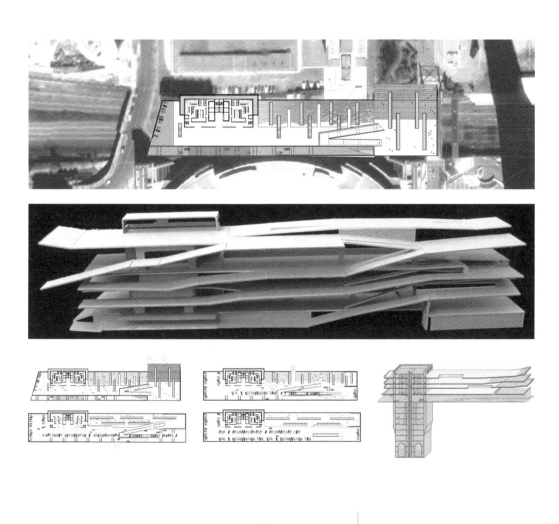

precipitation mm/total snow/temperature celsius

extreme maximum temperature °C
extreme minimum temperature °C
total precipitation mm
total snow cm

TORONTO, LESTER B PEARSON AIRPORT, 2006

Seventh Floor Ground on Hydro Block site

Liam Woofter

Seventh Floor Ground by Liam Woofter reclines a shallow basin alongside the office and hospital room windows that line University Avenue. Microscale fibre-reinforced concrete, which is almost bendable, looks like regular concrete but is 500 times more resilient to cracking and 40 percent lighter in weight, is used to articulate a precarious, plastic ramped palestra that stitches together various city elements. This unprepossessing, therapeutic space of refuge offers a partially enclosed pool structure, designed to resist and deflect high winds caused by the wind-tunnel effect, and utilizes impervious concrete to resist unwanted water penetration. For impervious concrete, the concrete is impregnated throughout its thickness and the sealer becomes a permanent part of the concrete so that it is unaffected by surface abrasion.

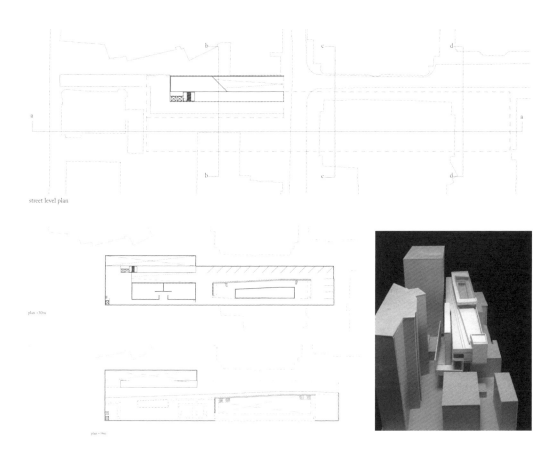

street level plan

plan +30m

plan +14m

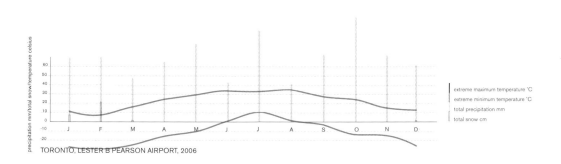

extreme maximum temperature ˚C
extreme minimum temperature ˚C
total precipitation mm
total snow cm

precipitation mm/total snow/temperature celsius

TORONTO, LESTER B PEARSON AIRPORT, 2006

Gardin Fronts on Gardiner Expressway site

Eric Van Ziffle

Gardin Fronts by Eric Van Ziffle creates a new buttress to the revered 1960s Gardiner Expressway – a raised concrete roadway that still supports a steady stream of commuter cars parallel to the City's somewhat forgotten waterfront. Foreign Office Architects' Phylogenesis strategy is reinterpreted to inhabit the super-thin concrete housing for a car rental/auto park/bus station structure at the edge of the raised expressway. It ultimately creates an artificial ecology, a series of "lungs", where cars' CO2 is consumed by vegetation, which in turn excretes O2 into the air. Organized as a coupled ramp system, centre hollows and staggered floor plates give relief to an otherwise lightless, deep and compressed concrete parking garage.

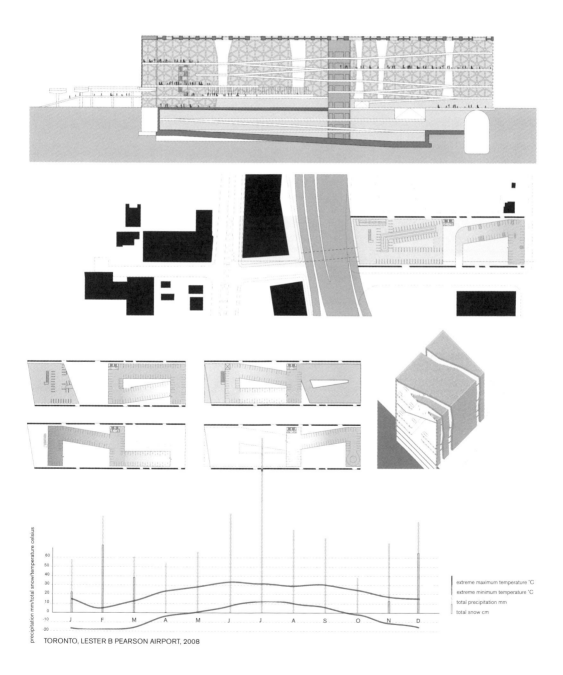

TORONTO, LESTER B PEARSON AIRPORT, 2008

extreme maximum temperature ˚C
extreme minimum temperature ˚C
total precipitation mm
total snow cm

precipitation mm/total snow/temperature celsius

Broken-Rib Panel, Toronto City Hall

Individually shaped white precise concrete
units render a glass cube organic.

afterword:
brutal memories

Charles Waldheim

For a generation of architects educated on the perceived 'failures' of modernist architecture, concrete became a dirty word. In my own experience as a student and young architect in the late 80s and early 90s the entire edifice of architectural culture seemed committed to redeeming itself from the sins of our fathers (and grandfathers) who brought forth a new image of urbane public building in concrete.

Growing up in the south, well outside the centres of production and consumption of architectural culture, I had my first encounter with architecture when I bumped into it and it made me bleed, literally. My first truly memorable architectural experience, the one that first really impressed upon me the potential for architecture as a medium of spatial and social liberation, was made of concrete. Not just any concrete, not the seemingly limitless, inexpensive, and generic light grey liquid of obscure origin that was constructing entire new neighbourhoods and lifestyles. No, not that rolling reservoir of unlimited availability evidenced in truck after truck across the region, but rather a specifically dark, rough, deliberately dangerous, and (I would later learn) brutalist-inspired approximation of stone. That I had never experienced a public building properly dressed in stone was no impediment to my experience of one meant to replace it. My first formative architectural experience, not the abstraction of the profession or the idea of being an architect, but rather my first profoundly phenomenal experience of a considered and well-crafted piece of architecture was of the public library in my hometown. This is probably not remarkable given the historical locus of architectural attention on the library as a public building, nor is it unique in the experience of architects. What is perhaps worth remarking upon, however, is how quickly the cultural and stylistic vagaries of architectural production now oscillate. By the time the Orlando Public Library was built (1966) it was representative of a style already rapidly falling out of fashion. Yet it was well ahead of the cultural curve for the south of the era. By the time I encountered it as a boy of five or six years, the building had weathered slightly and darkened. But its rough edges had not softened much because I can remember distinctly rounding a corner on the stair too quickly and scraping my otherwise undamaged elbow. But more than the physical sensation of rough board-formed concrete on skin, the building represented a kind of spatial and bodily liberation. Apart from the occasional moment of emancipation outside the fitting room of a department store, in the crowd of a sporting event, or on the edge of the woods near my house, it was in that library's enormous double height spaces stacked upon one another that I first enjoyed the spatial freedom to roam through public realm unmolested, and sufficiently removed from my mother's watchful eyes to feel alone in the city. On those early trips to the library with my mom, and on dozens of subsequent trips when I was sufficiently developed to self-organize my trip, I would return again and again to the plastic spatial organization of the library, its wonderfully rich textured walls, and the marvelously challenging rise and run of its multiple public stairs. I learned later in my education to be distrustful of such a direct and unmediated joy in the context of the expression of concrete, but as a boy, the dark, cool, secret interior of the stacks of the library were the closest I would come to a perfect world. Outside, and extending in all directions, the city was in constant construction, under a blaring southern sun. The generic equivalent of the library's building material was rapidly being poured night and day to build Disney World as well as the highways that took us to it, and the very driveways, carports, patios, and houses that circumscribed our suburban existence. The library's architect, John Johansen, I would later learn, was a second row contributor to the American (neo)brutalist moment. He was educated at Harvard with Gropius and worked closely with a series of modernist masters before settling in New Canaan, Connecticut and teaching at Yale. Given his Harvard and Yale experiences, he would have been an attentive observer of the completion of two major works of American brutalism, Le Corbusier's Carpenter Center at Harvard and Paul Rudolph's Art and Architecture Building at Yale, both completed in 1963, just as Johansen received the commission for the Orlando Public Library. Eschewing any overt historic references or admissions of precedent, Johansen was characteristically clear and direct with his prose, describing his building as simply "a composition in monolithic concrete."

This publication is a timely and well-conceived generational rebuttal to the arguments against modernism and its aspiration to articulate public buildings in concrete. Concrete is a material, as is evident in this collection, of extraordinary range and invention. In the hands of a skilled architect, it transcends its mundane profile in favor of a supple and resilient expression. It has been for far too long abused, as if its material identity alone could somehow stand in for the loss of the public realm, our faith in institutions, and the entire cultural load of the western tradition. As with many of the defining myths of postmodernism, this particular mythology, that concrete is incompatible with urbane, public, and civic contents, must surely be dispelled by now, as we once again confront the challenges of the modern world after the 'semantic nightmare' and its conflation of material, meaning, and memory.

FibreC by Rieder Smart Elements

appendix

editor/contributor biographies

Pina Petricone, *Editor*

Pina Petricone is an associate professor of architecture at the University of Toronto where she also holds the position of Director of the Master of Architecture Program since 2008. Pina shares her time as principal, with partner Ralph Giannone, of Giannone Petricone Associates Inc. Architects (GPAIA) in Toronto. Her work and research is preoccupied with questions of material culture and the city and is enriched by the overlapping complexities of professional practice, academic speculation, and teaching. Her work has been published widely and has received numerous awards mostly in recognition for its experimentation at the scale of the city and the manifestation of such at the scale of the tectonic detail. This range was recently featured in two anthologies: *Design City* (John Wiley & Sons: Great Britain, 2007) and *Details in Architecture: Creative Detailing by Leading Architects* (Images Publishing: Australia, 2009). Pina received a Master of Architecture II from Princeton University in 1995, and a Bachelor of Architecture from the University of Toronto in 1991.

Contributors:

George Baird

George Baird is the former Dean (2004-2009) of the John H. Daniels Faculty of Architecture, Landscape, and Design and Professor of Architecture at the University of Toronto. Prior to this he was the G. Ware Travelstead Professor of Architecture at the Graduate School of Design, Harvard University, where he acted as Director of the Master of Architecture Program and continued as partner of Baird Sampson Neuert Architects. His architecture and urban design firm has received numerous design awards, including Canadian Architect Magazine Awards and Governor General's Medals in Architecture. Baird has authored numerous publications and has lectured widely throughout the world. Most recently, his research in architectural theory has focused on the political and social status of urban public space and on debates revolving around 'critical architecture.' He is co-editor (with Charles Jencks) of *Meaning in Architecture* (1969), and (with Mark Lewis) of *Queues Rendezvous, Riots* (1995). He is also the author of *Alvar Aalto* (1969) as well as *The Space of Appearance* (1995). Baird is a member of the Royal Canadian Academy of Arts and a recipient of the Toronto Arts Foundation's Architecture and Design Award (1992) as well as the da Vinci Medal of the Ontario Association of Architects (2000). He is a Fellow of the Royal Architectural Institute of Canada, and in 2010 received the RAIC Gold Medal. In June 2011, George Baird received a Doctor of Engineering Degree from the University of Waterloo.

Will Bruder

Self-trained as an architect, Will Bruder has a Bachelor of Fine Arts degree in sculpture from the University of Wisconsin-Milwaukee. Following a full architectural apprenticeship under Gunnar Birkerts and Paolo Soleri, Will opened his own Phoenix based practice in 1974. Among the 500 completed commissions are the now iconic Deer Valley Rock Arts Center (1994), the Scottsdale Museum of Contemporary Art (1999), the Phoenix Central Library (2001), and more recently the Agave Branch Library (2006). Will's architecture has been widely published in more than 1,000 books and periodicals in the United States, Europe, and Japan. He has won more than 70 awards, including the Governor's Art Award 2004 and the Chrysler Design Award 2000. Will has recently taught at Yale University, University of Virginia, Washington University, M.I.T., and the University of Toronto's John H. Daniels Faculty of Architecture, Landscape, and Design as the 2006 Frank Gehry International Visiting Chair in Architecture.

George Elvin

George Elvin received a PhD in Architecture from the University of California at Berkeley in 1998 after running his own design-build firm for twelve years in Washington DC. In 2005 he held a Visiting Research Fellowship at the Institute for Advanced Study in the Humanities at the University of Edinburgh, working on his study "Small Plans: Nanotechnology, Architecture, and the Future of the Built Environment." Dr. Elvin is a Senior Research Associate at the Building Futures Institute and Associate Professor at the College of Architecture and Planning at Ball State University. His research on nanotechnology, wearable computers, and other innovative design technologies has been widely published. Dr. Elvin is president of Nanosearch, a nanotechnology research and advisory firm, author of nanotechbuzz.com, a leading nanotechnology weblog, and Director of Green Technology Forum, a leading research firm focusing on emerging green technologies for sustainable business.

Sarah Iwata

Sarah Iwata completed her Master of Architecture at the University of Toronto's John H. Daniels Faculty of Architecture, Landscape, and Design in 2006, when she was the recipient of the Heather Reisman Gold Medal in Design for her thesis work investigating the effects of concrete microclimate and its implications on the sustainable architectural envelope. Currently, she lives and works in Lethbridge, Alberta.

Jürgen Mayer H.

Jürgen Mayer H. of the firm J. Mayer H. Architects established in Berlin in 1996, has won numerous awards and competitions resulting in an impressive portfolio of built public projects and spaces, including: the Metropol Parasol in Seville (completed 2011); Mensa Karlsruhe (completed in 2006); the Plaza de la Encarnacion in Seville (completed in 2007); the Hasselt Stationsomgeving in Belgium (2005); and the An der Alster office complex in Hamburg (2005). Professor Mayer has taught at numerous schools in Europe and North America and was the first Europe-based architect to hold the Frank Gehry Chair International Visiting Chair at the University of Toronto's John H. Daniels Faculty of Architecture, Landscape & Design in 2008.

Graeme Stewart

Graeme Stewart is an Associate with the Toronto firm ERA Architects, and is the co-editor of *Concrete Toronto: A Guidebook to Concrete Architecture from the Fifties to the Seventies*. His international research and thesis work was instrumental in founding the Tower Renewal Project; an initiative in modern heritage examining the future of Toronto's remarkable stock of modern tower neighbourhoods with the City of Toronto, Province of Ontario, University of Toronto, and other partners. Graeme is a regular lecturer in the Toronto Area's Universities and Colleges and has been a sessional instructor at the Daniels Faculty of Architecture at the University of Toronto. Graeme is also a director of the Centre for Urban Growth and Renewal (CUG+R), an urban research organization formed by ERA and planning Alliance in 2009. In 2010, he was recipient of an RAIC National Urban Design Award.

Charles Waldheim

Charles Waldheim is Professor of Landscape Architecture and Chair of the Department of Landscape Architecture program at Harvard University's Graduate School of Design. His research focuses on contemporary urbanism and its relation to landscape. Waldheim coined the term 'landscape urbanism' to describe emerging design practices in the context of North American urbanism and has written extensively on the positions, practices, and precedents of the topic. He has lectured all over the world on the subject, and is perhaps best known for his book *The Landscape Urbanism Reader* (Princeton Architectural Press, 2006), the definitive account of this disciplinary realignment, which cites the city of Detroit as the most legible example of urban industrial economy in North America. Professor Waldheim has taught at various schools in Europe and North America and in 2006 received the Rome Prize from the American Academy in Rome.

Mark West

Mark West holds a degree from The Cooper Union for the Advancement of Art and Science and has completed post professional studies at The University of California Santa Cruz and Carlton University in Ottawa. Mark is the Founding Director of CAST (the Centre for Architectural Structures and Technologies) based at the University of Manitoba, where he is currently a Professor of Architecture. He has received wide recognition for his work as well as grants from The Canada Foundation for Innovation and The National Endowment for the Arts, among many others. Current research projects include the design and production of pre-cast fabric-formed concrete structures, compression vault and shell panels, and the construction of the first fabric formed building.

Studio Project Contributions by Daniels Graduates:

Gary Chien
Tangie Genshorek
Vanessa Graham
Jessie Grebenc
Jennifer Haliburton
Leigh Jeneroux
Shirley Lee
Anne Miller
Shi Ning
Alessia Soppelsa
Kenzie Thompson
Eric Van Ziffle
Liam Woofter

image credits

appendix

First published in the United Kingdom in 2012 by
Thames & Hudson Ltd, 181A High Holborn,
London WC1V 7QX

Original Edition published in The United States in 2011 by Oscar Riera Ojeda Publishers

Text copyright © 2011 by Pina Petricone
Design and layout copyright © 2011 by Oscar Riera Ojeda Publishers
Editorial Direction: Oscar Riera Ojeda
Managing Editors: Sarah Iwata and Alessia Soppelsa
Creative Direction: Leo Malinow
Graphic Design: Alejandra Román
Book Design Consultant: Anita Matusevics, Wonder Inc.
Copy Editing: Kit Maude
Cover Photograph: Gilberto Prioste

www.oscarrieraojeda.com
info@oscarrieraojeda.com

British Library Cataloguing-in-Publication Data
A catalogue record for this book is available from the British Library

ISBN: 978-0-500-34281-7

Printed and bound in China

To find out about all our publications, please visit **www.thamesandhudson.com** There you can subscribe to our e-newsletter, browse or download our current catalogue, and buy any titles that are in print.

RATP Bus Centre in Thiais, France,
by ECDM.